TRUTH
or DARE?
Do You Have the Courage
to Change Your Life?

TRUTH
or DARE?
Do You Have the Courage
to Change Your Life?

Tanja Crouch

First Printing: March, 2003

International Standard Book Number:

0-88290-736-0

Horizon Publishers' Catalog and Order Number:

1102

Printed and distributed
in the United States of America by

Horizon Publishers
& Distributors, Incorporated

Mailing Address:
P.O. Box 490
Bountiful, Utah 84011-0490

Street Address:
50 South 500 West
Bountiful, Utah 84010

Local Phone: (801) 295-9451
Toll Free: 1 (866) 818-6277
FAX: (801) 295-0196

E-mail: horizonp@burgoyne.com
Website: http://www.horizonpublishersbooks.com

Contents

Acknowledgments

The idea for this book came to me during the 2000 Christmas holiday. I knew then that the suggestion was an inspired gift. The process of researching and writing has been a joyful experience. Before writing each section, I got on my knees and asked Heavenly Father for help. I returned to my knees often, asking Him for further assistance, or to thank Him for continued inspiration. I am forever grateful for the blessing writing this book has been and hope that it will touch the hearts of those who read it.

I am grateful for the youth in the Franklin, Hopkinsville, Nashville, and Puducah Stakes who have changed my heart and brought meaning to my life. It is a privilege to have served as a teacher in Sunday School, Young Women, and Seminary. I particularly want to thank the following youth for their example and love: Scott Allen, Ashley Brickel, Scott Collins, Katharine Dinwiddie, Diane Dixon, Eric Ellsworth, Mark Foerster, Scott Foerster, Chris Harris, Randi Harris, Jon Hekking, Scott Hotard, Steven Hotard, Ryan Huish, Wren Hunter, Hollie Johnson, Amy Linder, Sarah Linder, Mindy Nabrotzky, Ricky Parris, Art Peach, Brad Peterson, Kristin Peterson, Alexis Price, Clint Proctor, Keri Reed, Vickie Rosa, Ashley Savarda, Rachel Settle, Emily Scruggs, Todd Soderquist, Diana Stucki, Eric Thomas, Travis Thurman, Danielle Watson, Jesse Welsh, Sierra Westfall, David Williamson, Diane Williamson, Kiel Wilson, Christie Winborn, and Jessica Winborn. I love each of you and am so grateful that Heavenly Father put you in my life.

Thank you Susan and Jay Yates for your love and prayers; and thanks to Betty Collins, Anne Dixon, Rebecca Frazier, Katie Minor, Tami Peterson, Dave Watson, and Mark Welsh for your kindness, example and influence in my life.

My agent, Diedre Knight, at The Knight Agency, is a gift from God: thank you for your time, love, and prayers.

Thank you to my family for their continued love, support and prayers: Luana Peck, Jim and Linda Peck, Dustin, Stacy, and Braden Peck, Denny and Carolyn Peck, Heather, Jason, Jeana, and Kevin Peck, Earlene Crouch, Jody and Stephen Williams, Rob and Georgia Crouch, Kevin, Danielle, Bryan, and Camille Crouch, Julie and David Ashby, Amanda, Michael, and Lindsey Ashby, and Dolores DeSpain. I could not have completed this book without my husband, best friend, and love: "The Kev."

Above all, I must acknowledge my Heavenly Father for his daily blessings and love, and Jesus Christ for his example and love. I know they live. I know that my prayers are heard and answered.

This book is dedicated in loving memory of:

Charles W. Peck, October 20, 1918-February 25, 1997
Robert B. Crouch, July 23, 1925-April 14, 2002

Introduction

Every change in life begins as a thought before being translated into action, and thus becoming a part of our life. In the Book of Mormon we read that following a period of great wickedness, Alma the younger experienced a profound change of heart (see Mosiah 27). While serving as the first chief judge in the land, he came to realize that in order for people to fully live the gospel, they too must first have a change of heart and be spiritually reborn.

Alma gave up his position as chief judge to devote himself to magnifying his calling of high priest. Instead of dealing with the final outcome of people's actions, he would work to bring about a change in their hearts, which had the power to affect their actions (see Alma 4 and 5).

Speaking of the change that comes from within, President Ezra Taft Benson stated: "The Lord works from the inside out. The world works from the outside in . . . The world would mold men by changing their environment. Christ changes men, who then change their environment. The world would shape human behavior, but Christ can change human nature."[1]

Based on the principle of combining spiritual thinking with action, *Truth or Dare* adapts the childhood game to deliver a unique aid to help Latter-day Saints examine what they know in their heart to be true, and to evaluate whether their daily acts support those truths. Then it challenges them to live a life that reflects their beliefs.

Playing the game of "truth or dare" requires courage to honestly answer the question posed or to accept the dare. The answers and actions are sometimes embarrassing, frustrating, awkward, uncomfortable and humorous. It requires even greater courage to accept the

---

1. Ezra Taft Benson, "Born of God," *Ensign*, Nov. 1985, 5.

challenges put forth in the book *Truth or Dare,* but the rewards can be eternal.

Each set of pages in a chapter presents both a truth and a dare. Selecting the truth, asks you to search your heart for what you truly believe or how you assess your actions regarding that principle, then asks you to answer the question honestly. If you select a dare, you are challenged to put the principle into practice in some specific ways. To deepen the process of examining the challenges, a mini-lesson is provided for each topic, containing stories and quotes from scriptures, prophets, apostles, general authorities, and other sources.

As each of us is at a different level in our spiritual progress, *Truth or Dare* was devised to be used in three different ways: (1) You can work through all of the truths, one after another, until you reach the end of the book, then work through each challenge; (2) You can work though the truths and the corresponding challenges together; or (3) You can randomly select a truth or a dare each time you pick up the book. These three options enable you to tailor the use of the book to guide your individual spiritual progress.

We are all looking for ways to become more in tune with the Spirit and live a righteous life worthy of returning to Heavenly Father's presence. Using spiritual principles to guide our thoughts and actions can bring joy and happiness into our lives and bring us closer to Him. *Truth or Dare* emphasizes the fact that the mind and body must act together to effect lasting change. Getting in touch with our thoughts and connecting them to our actions will result in a life filled with joy and blessings untold.

Truth or Dare—Do You Have the Courage to Change Your Life?

Chapter 1

Seeing the Divine Worth of Others

Your Personal Truth

- Do you believe that all people have the potential for good?
- Do you treat all people as if they are children of God?
- Can people change for the better when other people believe in them?
- Is humility required to help another realize their potential?

"Treat a man as he is and he will remain as he is. Treat a man as he can and should be, and he will become as he can and should be," wrote German poet and intellectual Johann Wolfgang von Goethe.

This fact is exemplified in a story of Sister Emma Ray Riggs McKay, wife of President David O. McKay. When she began teaching school, the principal introduced her to the class. As he did, "he pointed to a certain boy and said he was a troublemaker. She sensed the boy's embarrassment and feared he would live up to his reputation, so she wrote a note and slipped it to him as she passed his desk. It said, 'Earl, I think the principal was mistaken about your being a bad boy. I trust you, and know that you are going to help me make this room the best in the school.' Earl not only became a paragon of scholastic virtue, but also one of the town's most important people."[1]

The Book of Mormon account of Nephi's broken bow is another beautiful example of treating an individual as if he were what he should be, and seeing him rise to the occasion. Lehi's family pitched their tents in the wilderness and Nephi went out to slay food. Disastrously, he broke his bow, rendering him unable to obtain food. Laman and Lemuel murmured, as always, and for the first and only

---

1. N. Eldon Tanner, "Judge Not, That Ye Be Not Judged," *Ensign,* July 1972, 34.

time recorded, even father Lehi complained. Lehi was still the prophet, but he was old and Nephi had already been designated by the Lord to succeed him. Nephi had already seen angels and talked with the Spirit of the Lord. He had exhibited great strength and leadership. With his father wavering, he could have easily stepped forward and taken control. Instead, Nephi made a new bow and an arrow, and armed himself with a sling and stones before going to his father and asking, "Whither shall I go to obtain food?" Nephi could have easily inquired of the Lord himself, but he recognized the greatness in his father and wanted him to be strong again. (see 1 Nephi 16:18-39)

Speaking of this story, Elder Marion D. Hanks said: "A son who had strength enough, and humility enough, and manliness enough to go to his wavering superior and say, 'You ask God, will you?' because somehow he knew this is how you make men strong, that wise confidence in men builds them. Lehi asked God and God told him, and Lehi's leadership was restored."[2]

Each of us comes to mortality with the potential to achieve godhood. Each of us is literally the offspring of divinity. As we strive to become more like God, it is incumbent upon us to reach out, uplift, build, restore, and see the divine worth of our brothers and sisters. President Gordon B. Hinckley has said, "Under the sacred and compelling trust we have as members of the Church of Jesus Christ, ours is a work of redemption, of lifting and saving those who need help. Ours is a task of raising the sights of those of our people who fail to realize the great potential that lies within them."[3]

Robert Browning wrote: "I judge people by what they might be—not are, nor will be."[4]

Do you possess the humility to help others achieve their potential?

2. Marion D. Hanks, "Steps to Learning," *Brigham Young University Speeches of the Year,* 4 May 1960, 7.
3. Gordon B. Hinckley, "What This Work Is All About," *Ensign,* November 1982, 7.
4. Robert Browning, *A Soul's Tragedy.* Act ii.

Seeing the Divine Worth of Others

Dares to Improve Your Life

- I dare you to pray for your eyes to be opened to see the divine potential of others.

- For today, I dare you to treat each person you come in contact with as a child of God, with the potential for exaltation.

- For a week, a month, a year, or a lifetime, I dare you to pray for ways you can help your family members recognize their divine potential, and to have the courage to act on the inspiration that follows.

- I dare you to write a letter, make a phone call, ask for a blessing, offer encouragement—do something for someone that manifests your love and belief in their divine potential.

The conversion of Saul of Tarsus, a man famous for persecuting Christians, is a miraculous example of an individual coming to realize his potential. Neither Saul, nor anyone who knew him, would have described him as "chosen"—at least not based on his early conduct. But the Lord knew his divine potential. After seeing the Savior and learning that he was a chosen vessel, Saul was instantly converted and became a new man (see Acts 9). Saul changed his name to Paul, and grew to become one of the great Apostles of Jesus Christ.

"When the Savior called His disciples He was not looking for men and women of status, property, or fame," taught President James E. Faust. "He was looking for those of worth and potential. They were an interesting group, those early disciples: the fishermen, the tax gatherer, and the others."[1]

---

1. James E. Faust and James P. Bell, *In the Strength of the Lord: The Life and Teachings of James E. Faust* (Salt Lake City: Deseret Book Co., 1999), 425.

The Lord knows the divine worth of each of His children and stands ready to help us realize it. As we draw closer to Him, our eyes see clearer the potential of our brothers and sisters. It is our responsibility to help them both recognize it and achieve it. The Lord commanded, "succor the weak, lift up the hands which hang down, and strengthen the feeble knees" (D&C 81:5).

President Ezra Taft Benson told of an actual experience than illustrates how this principle can be applied. A young man of eighteen had come to him requesting a blessing to assist in working out some problems. President Benson asked if he would consider asking his father, an inactive Elder, to give the blessing. "When I asked, 'Do you love your father?' he replied, 'Yes, Brother Benson, he is a good man. I love him.' He then said, 'He doesn't attend to his priesthood duties as he should. He doesn't go to church regularly, I don't know that he is a tithe payer, but he is a good man, a good provider, a kind man.' I said, 'How would you like to talk to him at an opportune time and ask him if he would be willing to give you a father's blessing?'"

The young man expressed his reservations, but President Benson challenged him to try and promised he would pray for him. A few days later he returned and said, "'Brother Benson, that's the sweetest thing that has happened in our family.' He could hardly control his feelings as he told me what had happened. He said, 'When the opportunity was right, I mentioned it to Father, and he replied, 'Son, do you really want me to give you a blessing?' I told him, 'Yes, Dad, I would like you to.' Then he said, "Brother Benson, he gave me one of the most beautiful blessings you could ever ask for. Mother sat there crying all during the blessing. When he got through there was a bond of appreciation and gratitude and love between us that we have never had in our home."[2]

"Never give up on anybody. Miracles happen every day."[3]

Is there a potential miracle that needs your attention?

---

2. Ezra Taft Benson, "A Message to the Rising Generation," *Ensign,* November 1977, 30.

3. H. Jackson Brown, Jr., *Life's Little Instruction Book,* (Nashville, Tennessee: Rutledge Hill Press, 1991), #43.

Chapter 2

Open the Windows of Heaven

Your Personal Truth

- Are you stealing from your Heavenly Father?
- When you pay tithing, do you believe you are giving God a gift?
- How does paying tithing show your love for Heavenly Father?
- Are you a full and honest tithe payer?

It began with a few coins missing from mother's purse. Then a dollar or two was taken from father's wallet. Over time, the amounts increased and became more regular—someone was stealing from mother and father. The parents were heart broken when they discovered their own son, whom they had given everything to, including life itself, had stolen money from them. Imagine their pain.

When we do not pay a full and honest tithe, ten percent of our gross income (see D&C 199:4), we are literally stealing from our Father in Heaven who has given all things to us, including life itself. The prophet Malachi asked: "Will a man rob God? Yet ye have robbed me. But ye say, Wherein have we robbed thee? In tithes and offerings" (Malachi 3:8-12).

All that we have belongs to God. Tithing is not a gift we graciously give—it belongs to our Father in Heaven. President N. Eldon Tanner further explained this fact: "I often wonder if we realize that paying our tithing does not represent giving gifts to the Lord and the Church. Paying tithing is discharging a debt to the Lord. The Lord is the source of all our blessings, including life itself. The payment of tithing is a commandment, a commandment with a promise. If we obey this commandment, we are promised that we will 'prosper in the land.' This prosperity consists of more than material goods—it may

15

include enjoying good health and vigor of mind. It includes family solidarity and spiritual increase. I hope those of you not presently paying your full tithe will seek the faith and strength to do so. As you discharge this obligation to your Maker, you will find great, great happiness, the like of which is known only by those who are faithful to this commandment."[1]

When we return to the Lord one-tenth of what He has given us, we obey His commandment, and by so doing, prove our love for Him: "If ye love me, keep my commandments" (John 14:15).

Elder Bernard P. Brockbank once shared this testimony of tithing when his family was young: "We were struggling to meet our financial needs, and we were in debt, and we were not honest in our payment of tithes and offerings. We were attending church and I thought that we loved the Lord, but one day my wife said to me, 'Do you love God?' and I answered, 'Yes.' She said, 'Do you love God as much as you love the grocer?' I replied, 'I hope that I love him more than the grocer.' She said, 'But you paid the grocer. Do you love God as much as the landlord? You paid him, didn't you?'

She then said, 'The first and great commandment is to love God, and you know we have not paid our tithing.' We repented and paid our tithes and offerings, and the Lord opened the windows of heaven and poured out blessings upon us. We consider it a great privilege to pay tithes and offerings to the Lord."[2]

Do you love your Father in Heaven enough to be an honest tithe payer?

---

1. N. Eldon Tanner, "Constancy Amid Change," *Ensign*, Nov. 1979, 80.
2. Bernard P. Brockbank, "Love of God," *Ensign*, June 1971, 85.

Open the Windows of Heaven

Dares to Improve Your Life

- I dare you to pray for a testimony of tithing.
- I dare you to pay your tithing before you pay any other debt.
- I dare you to pay a full and honest tithe.
- I dare you to bear your testimony of the law of tithing.

Tithing is a fundamental law of the gospel of Jesus Christ, necessary for exaltation. A member must be a full tithe payer to receive a temple recommend, and therefore to receive the ordinances, blessings and covenants necessary for exaltation. Elder Hartman Rector, Jr. testified of this fact: "If a man were to keep all of the Lord's commandments with the exception of tithing, he still could never be married for time and all eternity in the temple . . . Without tithing there is no exaltation. As we think about it, we know this is true."[1]

While great blessings are promised to those who abide by the law, obedience is required first: "There is a law, irrevocably decreed in heaven before the foundations of this world, upon which all blessings are predicated—and when we obtain any blessing from God, it is by obedience to that law upon which it is predicated" (D&C 130:21).

Whether it is to receive the ordinances of the temple or the outpouring of the blessings of heaven, obedience and faith precede the miracle. President Spencer W. Kimball explained: "In faith we plant the seed, and soon we see the miracle of the blossoming. Men have often misunderstood and have reversed the process. They would have the harvest before the planting, the reward before the service, the miracle before the faith. Even the most demanding labor unions would hardly ask the wages before the labor. But many of us would have the

---

1. Hartman Rector, Jr., "That Ye May Have Roots and Branches," *Ensign*, May 1983, 25.

vigor without the observance of the health laws, prosperity through the opened windows of heaven without the payment of our tithes. We would have the close communion with our Father without fasting and praying; we would have rain in due season and peace in the land without observing the Sabbath and keeping the other commandments of the Lord. We would pluck the rose before planting the roots; we would harvest the grain before sowing and cultivating. . . ."[2]

Like all principles of the gospel, obedience to the law of tithing is a matter of faith. President Gordon B. Hinckley has said: "We take the Lord at His word, and it is my testimony that He keeps His word. It is He who made the promise. That is not my promise. It is His promise that He will open the windows of heaven and pour down blessings upon you which you will not have room enough to receive."[3]

Speaking of the blessings associated with the law of tithing, Elder Dallin H. Oaks shared: "Some people say, 'I can't afford to pay tithing.' Those who place their faith in the Lord's promises say, 'I can't afford not to pay tithing.'"[4]

Do you have the faith to receive an outpouring of blessings?

---

2. Spencer W. Kimball, *The Teachings of Spencer W. Kimball,* edited by Edward L. Kimball (Salt Lake City: Bookcraft, 1982), 54.
3. Gordon B. Hinckley, "Words of the Living Prophet," *Liahona,* February 1998, 12.
4. Dallin H. Oaks, "Tithing," *Ensign,* May 1994, 33.

Chapter 3

Under the Influence of Television

```
╔══════════════════════════════════════════════════╗
              Your Personal Truth

 • Do the television programs you watch support or attack
   what you believe is morally right?

 • Has a television program ever led you to become more
   accepting of immoral behavior and language?

 • Do the television programs you watch make you feel closer
   to God or to Satan?

 • Would you feel comfortable if the Savior sat down to watch
   your favorite television program with you?
╚══════════════════════════════════════════════════╝
```

Television is a powerful medium. In an instant we can bring the world into our homes. With a simple touch of the remote, we are exposed to sights and sounds that can inspire or demoralize.

Satan works to blur the distinction between the two. This is one of his cleverest tools: to gray the area between light and darkness. He entices us with television programs that initially seem entertaining and fun, but their storylines, characters and dialog are not in keeping with our moral standards. Satan wants us to tune in the most popular sitcom, drama, movie or news magazine and pacify ourselves that it must be good, to be so highly rated. Or justify our choices by saying, "the program puts forth a positive message," and try to ignore the fact that the characters are immoral, violent, or use offensive language.

Isaiah prophesied that ours was a time when men would "call evil good, and good evil; that put darkness for light, and light for darkness; that put bitter for sweet, and sweet for bitter!" (Isaiah 5:20).

Satan is a master at using this stratagem. He whispers to us, "It's okay, it's just a television show," and hopes we will justify inviting immorality, innuendo, lewd language and other corrupt behavior into our homes and minds, where they can make a lasting impression. He

19

wants us to believe that hearing the Lord's name repeatedly taken in vain by characters that joke about sexual situations and behave immorally, will not affect our spirit. But he knows it does.

Long after the program is over and the television is turned off, a memory of what was seen and heard remains logged in our brain and leaves a permanent mark on our spirit. James Allen wrote, "A man is literally what he thinks, his character being the complete sum of all his thoughts."[1] When we begin to grasp this concept, sinful impressions take on greater significance.

Hours and hours of good impressions will never fully erase evil sights and sounds. They must be turned away from. President Ezra Taft Benson directed us to "Avoid books, magazines, videos, movies, and television shows that are not good. As the scriptures tell us, avoid the very appearance of evil."[2]

If a program does not inspire and uplift your spirit, why give it your time and attention?

1. James Allen, *As A Man Thinketh*, (New York City: Barnes & Noble Books, 1992), 2.
2. Ezra Taft Benson, *Come, Listen to a Prophet's Voice* (Salt Lake City: Deseret Book Co., 1990), 66.

Under the Influence of Television

Dares to Improve Your Life

- I dare you to change the channel or turn off television programs that are not in keeping with your moral beliefs.
- I dare you to throw out videos that contain language and situations that are not in accordance with your value system.
- I dare you to write a letter or send an e-mail that praises quality, uplifting television content.
- I dare you to make a list of positive activities to do instead of watching television and keep it near the remote control or programming guide.

In a vision, Nephi was allowed to see our time and witnessed Satan's power to confound and delude the present generation. He warned us to guard ourselves against the Adversary's clever deceptions, saying, "And others will he pacify, and lull them away into carnal security, that they will say: All is well in Zion; yea, Zion prospereth, all is well—and thus the devil cheateth their souls, and leadeth them away carefully down to hell" (2 Nephi 28:21).

With each impression of wicked life-style and language, Satan cunningly "cheateth [our] souls, and leadeth [us]" to find these sinful situations less shocking, less offensive and less objectionable. Behavior that was once considered scandalous has become commonplace.

Journalist David Frost once joked about the negative influence of television saying, "[It] is an invention that permits you to be entertained in your living room by people you wouldn't have in your home."

Do you invite vulgar characters into your home and mind, where they can take up residence?

Alma understood the destructive effect of evil visual images. To his son Corianton, he warned, ". . . go no more after the lusts of your eyes . . ." (Alma 39:9). We must heed Alma's advice and turn off programs that are not in harmony with our values. We cannot allow immoral behavior and language to stain our homes and minds and spirits.

The apostle Paul personally experienced Satan's power to deceive and warned the Saints to shun his influence. In a letter to the Thessalonians, he wrote this simple and clear directive: "Abstain from all appearance of evil." (I Thessalonians 5:22.) The adversary knows if we trifle with evil, it will become less offensive. He hopes we are arrogant enough to believe we can handle exposure to immoral behavior and language that is disguised as entertainment, but we cannot.

"In a day when broadcasters and publishers have rather free access into our homes, we must seek clean, uplifting entertainment, on television and videos and in movies, magazines, books, and other printed material," counseled Elder Joseph B. Wirthlin. "We should be very selective and choose only those things that meet the test of being virtuous, lovely, of good report, or praiseworthy. If it is questionable, we should avoid it."[1]

Do your favorite television programs past the test of being "virtuous, lovely, or of good report or praiseworthy?" (see *Articles of Faith* 13).

---

1. Joseph B. Wirthlin, *Finding Peace in Our Lives* (Salt Lake City: Deseret Book Co., 1995), 134.

Chapter 4

Following The Prophet

Your Personal Truth

- Do you believe that God's living prophet is literally His mouthpiece?
- Do you sustain the First Presidency and Quorum of the Twelve as apostles and prophets?
- Do you know what the First Presidency message (printed in the *Ensign*) is this month?
- Can you name specific counsel the First Presidency and Quorum of the Twelve gave in the last General Conference?

"Have you ever had the experience of driving around and around the streets of a city with the driver saying, 'I know where it is; I'm sure I can find it'? Finally, in frustration, he stops and asks someone for directions. How much easier it is to find our way when we follow the directions of someone who knows how to locate our destination. These are difficult times. Is there one clear, unpolluted, unbiased voice that we can always count on? Is there a voice that will always give us clear directions to find our way in today's troubled world? The answer is yes," said Elder M. Russell Ballard. "That voice is the voice of the living prophet and apostles."[1]

Twice yearly, during General Conference, we are each given the opportunity to sustain the First Presidency and Quorum of the Twelve, whom the Lord has already called by revelation, as apostles and prophets. One of the dictionary definitions of the word "sustain" is "to uphold; to support" or "to maintain; to support; not to dismiss or abate."[2] By raising our arm to the square in sustaining the Lord's

---

1. M. Russell Ballard, "Follow the Prophet," *New Era*, September 2001, 4.
2. *An American Dictionary of the English Language*, (Noah Webster, 1828), electronic edition, © 1998 Deseret Book Company.

chosen, we make the action binding and covenant to "uphold, support, maintain" and "not to dismiss" their counsel.

Concerning the sustaining of leaders, President John Taylor once said: "We hold up our right hand . . . it is in token to God that we are sincere in what we do, and that we will sustain the parties we vote for . . . If we agree to do a thing and do not do it, we become covenant breakers and violators of our obligations, which are, perhaps, as solemn and binding as anything we can enter into."[3]

The Prophet is the mouthpiece of God. The Lord declared: "What I the Lord have spoken, I have spoken, and I excuse not myself; and though the heavens and the earth pass away, my word shall not pass away, but shall be fulfilled, whether by mine own voice or by the voice of my servants, it is the same" (D&C 1:38). If we profess to follow Christ, we must follow His chosen prophet.

While serving as President of the Quorum of the Twelve, President Ezra Taft Benson said: "The most important prophet, so far as we are concerned, is the one who is living in our day and age. This is the prophet who has today's instructions from God to us today. God's revelation to Adam did not instruct Noah how to build the ark. Every generation has need of the ancient scripture plus the current scripture from the living prophet. Therefore, the most crucial reading and pondering which you should do is of the latest inspired words from the Lord's mouthpiece. That is why it is essential that you have access to and carefully read his words in current Church publications."[4]

While serving in the Quorum of the Twelve, President Harold B. Lee said that the general conference report should "be the guide to [our] walk and talk during the next six months."[5]

Do you keep the covenant you made with God to sustain His prophet and apostles?

---

3. John Taylor, *Journal of Discourses,* 26 vols. (London: Latter-day Saints' Book Depot, 1854-1886), 2:207.
4. Ezra Taft Benson, *Conference Report,* Korea Area Conference 1975, 52.
5. Harold B. Lee, *Conference Report,* April 1946, 68.

Following The Prophet

> ## Dares to Improve Your Life
>
> - I dare you to subscribe to the *Ensign* and *Church News* (also, *New Era* and *Friend,* if younger adults and children are in the home). Commit to read at least one article each Sunday.
> - For the next six months, I dare you to read and study the current General Conference talks.
> - Each month, I dare you to read and study the First Presidency Message in the *Ensign* and *New Era.*
> - I dare you to select one specific thing the Prophet has recently instructed us to do and commit to work on it. Then select another . . .

Latter-day Saints express gratitude for a prophet in prayer, testimony and song. We proudly sing from memory: "We thank thee, O God, for a prophet, to guide us in these latter days."[1] Twice yearly, millions of members gather for General Conference in person, via satellite or the Internet to hear the prophet's voice. Yet, how many really listen? How grateful are we if we do not heed his counsel?

Satan uses pride, lack of faith, or apathy to dissuade us from heeding important counsel that will improve the quality of our mortal and eternal lives. Many are like Naaman of the Old Testament (see 2 Kings 5:1-14). A captain in the Syrian army, Naaman was a great and honorable man. He was also a leper. Naaman sought out the prophet Elisha to heal him from his leprosy. Arriving with a display of wealth and expecting a great miracle, Naaman was angered when the prophet sent one of his servants saying, "Go and wash in Jordan seven times, and thy flesh shall come again to thee, and thou shalt be clean" (2 Kings 5:10). Pride and stubbornness kept Naaman from receiving

---

1. *Hymns of The Church of Jesus Christ of Latter-Day Saints,* (Salt Lake City: The Church of Jesus Christ of Latter-day Saints, 1985), no. 19.

God's blessings through His prophet. Fortunately Naaman's wise servants convinced their master to heed the prophet's simple instructions and "his flesh came again like unto the flesh of a little child, and he was clean" (vs.14). How many of us miss out on great and promised blessings because we do not listen and then obey the relatively simple things our prophet is telling us today?

"It is no small thing to have a prophet of God in our midst," said Elder M. Russell Ballard. "Great and wonderful are the blessings that come into our lives as we listen to the word of the Lord given to us through him. At the same time, knowing that President Gordon B. Hinckley is God's prophet also endows us with responsibility. When we hear the counsel of the Lord expressed through the words of the President of the Church, our response should be positive and prompt."[2]

Do you pray daily as a family? Do you hold weekly Family Home Evening? Are you studying the Book of Mormon? Do you pay a full tithe and a generous fast offering? Do you study the General Conference talks, First Presidency Messages and other articles in the Church magazines?

In recent addresses, the Prophet Gordon B. Hinckley has said: "get free of debt and have a little laid aside" (*Ensign,* November 2001, 73), "we have been continuously counseled for more than 60 years, let us have some food set aside that would sustain us for a time" (*Ensign,* November 2001, 73), "Observe the Word of Wisdom" ("Converts and Young Men," *Ensign,* May 1997, 47; and insert *Ensign,* February 2002, 53). He has repeatedly spoken of the importance of regular temple worship.

In November of 2000, President Hinckley challenged the youth of the church to be grateful, be smart, be clean, be true, be humble, and be prayerful. The six "Bs," as he called them, should be a standard for all Latter-day Saints. (see Gordon B. Hinckley, "A Prophet's Counsel and Prayer for Youth," *Ensign,* January 2001, 2.)

President J. Reuben Clark, Jr., said, "We do not lack a prophet; what we lack is a listening ear."[3]

Do you listen and obey the counsel of the prophet–the word of God?

---

2. M. Russell Ballard, "Follow the Prophet," *New Era,* September 2001, 4.
3. J. Reuben Clark, Jr., *Conference Report,* October 1948, Second Day—Morning Meeting, 80.

Chapter 5

Willing to Serve

Your Personal Truth

- Do other people think of you as a good neighbor?
- What evidence is there that you love your fellowman?
- How is service to your fellowman service to God?
- What have you done to serve God today?

Service transforms people. With each deed rendered, two or more lives are changed: the server's and the one being served. Service refines and purifies. It uplifts the spirit by teaching us to focus less on our own situation and more on the needs of others. Compassionate service increases our spirituality and prepares us to be worthy to dwell in God's presence.

Each act of loving service draws us nearer to our Father in Heaven. Day by day, as we serve our fellowman, we are becoming more like Christ and Heavenly Father. President Spencer W. Kimball stated: "Perhaps the most essential godlike quality is that of compassion and love—compassion shown forth in service to others, unselfishness, that ultimate expression of concern for others we call love. Wherever our Father's children magnify their opportunities for loving service, they are learning to become more like Him."[1]

Our Savior Jesus Christ is the perfect example of compassionate and loving service, dedicating His life to the welfare of others. In the last hours before He would rescue all of mankind, He humbly knelt and washed His disciples' feet (see John 13:5). Our devotion to Heavenly Father and Jesus Christ is not measured by the grandness of our service, but by the depth of humility, compassion and love we give. "When I give," said poet Walt Whitman, "I give myself."

---

1. Spencer W. Kimball, "President Kimball Speaks Out on Service to Others," *New Era*, March 1981, 47.

Beloved King Benjamin's life exemplified selfless service and Christlike love. He humbly served his people with no thought of seeking wealth, freeing the oppressed, instituting laws and order, teaching the commandments of God, laboring for his own welfare, and establishing peace throughout the land (see Mosiah 2:11-14). Nearing the end of his life, this noble prophet-leader's final sermon taught in beautiful simplicity the doctrine of service. "I tell you these things that ye may learn wisdom; that ye may learn that when ye are in the service of your fellow beings, ye are only in the service of your God" (Mosiah 2:17).

"The Lord does notice us, and he watches over us," said President Kimball. "But it is usually through another person that he meets our needs. Therefore, it is vital that we serve each other. The righteous life is achieved as we magnify our view of life, and expand our view of others and of our own possibilities. Thus, the more we follow the teachings of the Master, the more enlarged our perspective becomes. We see many more possibilities for service than we would have seen without this magnification. There is great security in spirituality, and we cannot have spirituality without service!"[2]

Service is a talent to be cultivated and practiced daily: hold a door open for someone, give your seat to another, share some fresh baked cookies, rake some leaves, watch a neighbor's children, help someone with homework, take out the trash, perform temple work for the dead, drive someone to seminary, take someone's turn for the carpool, write to a missionary, make a call, lend a hand.

Each day, look for something that you can do to serve the needs of another—and then do it! Henry David Thoreau wrote, "If I can put one touch of a rosy sunset into the life of any man or woman, I shall feel that I have worked with God."

Have you worked with God today?

---

2. *Ibid.*

Willing to Serve

Dares to Improve Your Life

- Each day for a month, I dare you to pray for willingness to serve and the ability to recognize opportunities.

- I dare you to do something today that will make the world a better place to live. It may be as simple as picking up some trash from the sidewalk or as big as volunteering for a service project.

- Each day for a week, I dare you to perform an act of service for members of your family.

- Each day for a month, I dare you to perform a small act of service for a stranger.

Are you willing to write an uplifting note to someone whose spirit might be low? Are you willing to telephone or go see someone who might be lonely? Are you willing to volunteer for a service project? Are you willing to take a meal to someone who is ill? Are you willing to mow an elderly person's lawn? Are you willing to give a ride to someone whose car is in the garage for repairs? Are you willing to help do what needs to be done? The Lord needs willing disciples who are "not weary in well-doing" because "out of small things proceedeth that which is great" (D&C 64:33). In order to "eat the good of the land of Zion" He requires "heart and a willing mind" (D&C 64:34). His disciples are those who are willing to show up, see what needs to be done, and do it with a loving heart.

All of us have been blessed with differing talents, skills, and resources that can be used to benefit our fellowman. Speaking of the parable of the barren fig tree (see Matthew 21:19) which was cursed for its unproductiveness, President Spencer W. Kimball once said, "What a loss to the individual and to humanity if the vine does not grow, the tree does not bear fruit, the soul does not expand through service! One must live, not only exist; he must do, not merely be; he must grow, not just vegetate. We must use our talents in behalf of our fellowmen, rather than burying them in the tomb of a self-centered life. Personal purity and veracity and stability in leadership are essential if we are to give sanctified service to others. We must expend our energies and use our skills for purposes larger than our own self-interest if we desire true happiness."[1]

The Savior, whose life and death were devoted to the service of mankind, taught the first and second great commandments were to "love the Lord thy God with all thy heart, and with all thy soul, and with all thy strength, and with all thy mind; and thy neighbour as thyself." (Luke 10:27.) When asked, "who is my neighbour?" He responded by teaching the parable of the good Samaritan. Free from prejudice and excuse, the Samaritan possessed a heart willing to serve. "He had compassion" for the injured stranger and "bound up his wounds" and "took care of him" (see Luke 10:30-37).

"There are so many who have been hurt and injured and who need a good Samaritan to bind up their wounds and help them on their way," said President Gordon B. Hinckley. "A small kindness can bring a great blessing to someone in distress and a sweet feeling to the one who befriends him."[2]

The more we serve our fellowmen, "the more substance there is to our souls," taught President Kimball. "We become more significant individuals as we serve others. We become more substantive as we serve others—indeed, it is easier to "find" ourselves because there is so much more of us to find!"[1]

One man who wanted to find direction for his life, wanted to experience more joy in daily living, humbly knelt in prayer and asked Heavenly Father, "What would thou have me do? I am willing to do thy will, how can I serve thee?"

Are your mind, hands, and heart willing to serve?

---

1. Spencer W. Kimball, "President Kimball Speaks Out on Service to Others," *New Era*, March 1981, 47.
2. Gordon B. Hinckley, "A Conversation with Single Adults," *Ensign*, March 1997, 58.

Chapter 6

Fasting with a Purpose

Your Personal Truth

- Is fasting a good suggestion, or is it a commandment?
- Do you begin and close your fast with prayer?
- Do you fast with a purpose in mind?
- Do you use fasting to resolve problems and increase your spirituality?

Since the time of Adam and Eve, people have fasted to increase their faith, overcome adversity, solve problems, receive blessings, and strengthen their spiritual connection to God. At the beginning of the Savior's ministry, He fasted and prayed forty days and nights to learn the will of Heavenly Father and obtain the strength to do it (see Luke 4:1-2).

The powerful combination of fasting and prayer is exemplified by the sons of Mosiah. During their 14-year mission among the Lamanites they faced overwhelming trials and tribulations, yet they "waxed strong in the knowledge of the truth" and became "men of a sound understanding" because "they had searched the scriptures diligently, that they might know the word of God" and "they had given themselves to much prayer, and fasting" (Alma 17:2-3).

In answer to their fervent prayer and fasting, the Lord blessed them with strength to overcome adversity and gave them "the spirit of prophecy, and the spirit of revelation" so that "when they taught, they taught with power and authority of God" (Alma 17:3). As a result, they were instruments in bringing thousands of Lamanites to the knowledge of Christ.

The prophet Amaleki recognized the power and strength that could be gained from fasting and prayer. He exhorted his people to "continue in fasting and praying, and endure to the end; and as the Lord liveth ye will be saved" (Omni 1:26).

Through latter-day revelation given to the prophet Joseph Smith, we learn that the Lord still expects His people to fast and pray often: "I give unto you a commandment that ye shall continue in prayer and fasting from this time forth" (D&C 88:76).

While serving as Presiding Bishop, John H. Vandenberg said: "Fasting and prayer equip a person with a much greater degree of strength and power than would otherwise be his if he were left to his own devices. Fasting and prayer can bring an individual to a point of humility and faith where the Lord can give him the extra strength and power needed to complete a task or to solve a problem."[1]

Self-mastery of our appetites and desires strengthens our character, builds self-esteem and brings us closer to God. "If there were no other virtue in fasting but gaining strength of character, that alone would be sufficient justification for its universal acceptance," said President David O. McKay. "He who reigns within himself and rules passions, desires, and fears is more than king."[2]

What was the purpose of your last fast?

---

1. Bishop John H. Vandenberg, "The Presiding Bishop Talks to Youth About: Fasting," *Improvement Era,* February 1969, 71.
2. President David O. McKay, "Questions—and Faith," *Improvement Era,* July 1953, 7.

Fasting with a Purpose

Dares to Improve Your Life

- I dare you to begin and close your fast with humble prayer.
- I dare you to fast with a clear purpose in mind.
- I dare you to use fasting to resolve a specific problem or increase your spirituality.
- I dare you to examine how you prepare for fasting and determine what you can do to make it a more positive and uplifting experience.

Just as faith without works is dead, fasting without purpose brings no reward. It is just going hungry. Food becomes the focus of our attention. If we fast with a purpose, the reason for our fast is what we concentrate on. In a sense, we are hungry and thirsty for the spiritual nourishment that comes from our Heavenly Father.

The combining of fasting with prayer is significant when we realize our objective is to receive spiritual sustenance from God.

Throughout the scriptures, prayer and fasting are mentioned together. Alma said: "I have fasted and prayed many days that I might know these things of myself. And now I do know of myself that they are true; for the Lord God hath made them manifest unto me by his Holy Spirit" (Alma 5:46).

Joseph Smith taught that turning our minds away from worldly desire to focus on spiritual matters through fasting and prayer should be a joyful experience that brings us closer to God: "This is fasting and prayer, or in other words, rejoicing and prayer" (D&C 59:14).

If we obey God's commandment to fast and pray, President Joseph F. Smith promised, "this law would bring [us] nearer to God, and divert [our] minds once a month at least, from the mad rush of worldly affairs and cause [us] to be brought into immediate contact with practical, pure and undefiled religion—to visit the fatherless and the widow, and keep [our]selves unspotted from the sins of the world. For religion is not in believing the commandments only, it is in doing them."[1]

In order to receive the blessings promised, we must fast often with prayer and purpose.

Former Presiding Bishop John H. Vandenberg compared the combination of prayer and fasting to an athlete's getting his second wind. "Athletes often speak of gaining a second wind or receiving additional strength after they have given all they could. A basketball player, for example, who plays until he's extremely tired may either slow down or he can continue to play hard even though it may be extremely difficult for a time. If he chooses the latter and continues to play hard, he may gain his so-called second wind. This additional strength doesn't come, however, until the player puts forth all he can give, plus a little more."[2]

When we put forth "all [we] can give, plus a little more" the blessings are rich and eternal. Isaiah tells us that when we fast: "Then shall thy light break forth as the morning, and thine health shall spring forth speedily: and thy righteousness shall go before thee; the glory of the Lord shall be thy reward. Then shalt thou call, and the Lord shall answer; thou shalt cry, and he shall say, Here I am" (Isaiah 58:8-9).

Is it worth sacrificing a couple of meals to have the Lord with you?

When was the last time you fasted and called upon the Lord?

---

1. Joseph F. Smith, *Gospel Doctrine: Selections from the Sermons and Writings of Joseph F. Smith,* compiled by John A. Widtsoe, (Salt Lake City: Deseret Book Co., 1939), 237.
2. John H. Vandenberg, "Fasting," *Improvement Era,* February 1969, 71.

Chapter 7

Be Who You Are

Your Personal Truth

- Do you really believe that you are the literal offspring of God?
- Do you know that you personally have the potential to become a god or goddess, a joint-heir with Jesus Christ?
- Can having an eternal perspective help you endure difficult trials or make righteous decisions?
- Do you waste opportunities, or are you striving for excellence?

We share the earth with other noble princes and princesses whose potential, like our own, is beyond our mortal comprehension. We are temporarily afflicted with amnesia of our premortal greatness. It is vital, however, to our spiritual survival that we strive to catch a glimpse of our divine potential because it affects everything we think and do. Solomon proclaimed, "Where there is no vision, the people perish" (Proverbs 29:18).

An essential step toward improving our vision to see our divine potential is having faith in Heavenly Father and Jesus Christ, and knowing that we are literally the offspring of God, with the potential to become gods and goddesses, priests and priestesses. In order to claim our divine inheritance—to be "crowned with honor, and glory, and immortality, and eternal life" (D&C 75:5)—we must first believe it can be ours. If we will exercise faith and listen, "The Spirit itself [will bear] witness with our spirit, that we are the children of God: And if children, then heirs; heirs of God, and joint-heirs with Christ . . . glorified together" (Romans 8:16-17).

David clearly understood the vision of who he was and could become when he wrote: "When I consider thy heavens, the work of thy fingers, the moon and the stars, which thou hast ordained; What is man, that thou art mindful of him? and the son of man, that thou visitest him? For thou hast made him a little lower than the angels, and hast crowned him with glory and honour" (Psalms 8:3-5). We are the literal offspring of God with inherent Godly attributes.

President Gordon B. Hinckley has said: "We are all children of God, and there is something of His divinity within each of us. We are more than a son or daughter of Mr. and Mrs. So-and-So who reside in such-and-such a place. We are of the family of God, with such a tremendous potential for excellence. The distance between mediocrity and excellence can be ever so small . . . I want to invite us all to walk a higher road of excellence . . . I plead with you: don't be a scrub! Rise to the high ground of spiritual, mental, and physical excellence. You can do it. You may not be a genius. You may be lacking in some skills. But so many of us can do better than we are now doing. We are members of this great Church whose influence is now felt over the world. We are people with a present and with a future. Don't muff your opportunities. Be excellent."[1]

Do your achievements reflect your divine potential?

---

1. Gordon B. Hinckley, "The Quest for Excellence," *Ensign*, September 1999.

Be Who You Are

Dares to Improve Your Life

- I dare you to read Abraham 3 and ponder the events described.
- I dare you to memorize the words to "I Am A Child of God" and recall them in your mind or sing them aloud at least once each day for a week—or a month. Do it with conviction!
- I dare you to read your patriarchal blessing and write down specific insights into your divine character.
- Each day for a month, (or longer) I dare you to ask Heavenly Father to help you realize your divine potential.

We must become more of ourselves! It has been said: "No matter where you go, there you are." There is no escaping ourselves—we are there when we go to sleep at night, when we wake in the morning and all day long. With so much time spent with ourselves, we must use it wisely, and strive daily to become more of who we really are, "the offspring of God" (Acts 17:29) with the potential for exaltation.

Sister Sheri Dew, former Second Counselor in the Relief Society General Presidency, understands clearly who she is. She has challenged us to come to the same realization: "As a people, we talk and sing constantly about who we are. Three-year-olds know the words to 'I Am a Child of God.' The Proclamation on the Family declares that we each have a divine destiny. The second Young Women's value is divine nature. And the very first words in the Relief Society Declaration are, 'We are beloved spirit daughters of God, and our lives have meaning, purpose, and direction.' And yet, with all our talking, do we really believe? Do we really understand? Has this transcendent doctrine about who we are—meaning who we have always been and, therefore, who we may become—permeated our hearts?"[1]

---

1. Sheri Dew, "Knowing Who You Are—and Who You Have Always Been," address given at Brigham Young University General Women's Conference, May 2001.

Our spirits long for us to become more of who we are—"the noble and great ones . . ." who "keep [our] second estate" and "have glory added upon [our] heads for ever and ever" (Abraham 3:22, 26). Every thought, every action, every minute, we are becoming more or less of our divine selves.

President Gordon B. Hinckley know who he is and wants us to understand our divine heritage. He has stated: You are creatures of divinity; you are [sons and] daughters of the Almighty. Limitless is your potential. Magnificent is your future, if you will take control of it. Do not let your lives drift in a fruitless and worthless manner . . . Never forget that you came to earth as a child of the divine Father, with something of divinity in your very makeup. The Lord did not send you here to fail. He did not give you life to waste it. He bestowed upon you the gift of mortality that you might gain experience—positive, wonderful, purposeful experience—that will lead to life eternal."[2]

In the great counsel in heaven, before this world was created, we stood beside the Savior and endorsed God's plan of salvation. We were reserved for this time because we had the courage and determination to come into mortality to face the world at its worst. We are sons and daughters of royal birth.

Do you really know that you are the offspring of God?

---

2. Gordon B. Hinckley, "How Can I Become the Woman of Whom I Dream?," *Ensign*, May 2001, 93; and *New Era*, November 2001, 4.

Chapter 8

Truth, Honesty and Integrity

Your Personal Truth

- Are you honest with God, yourself and other people?
- Do you always keep your word?
- Are there degrees of honesty and integrity?
- Is your word as good as your bond?

"Rather than love, than money, than fame, give me truth," wrote Henry David Thoreau. What greater gift can we give to our family, to our fellowman, to ourselves and to God, than truth?

The Ten Commandments instruct: "Thou shalt not steal; Thou shalt not bear false witness; Thou shalt not covet" (Exodus 20:15-17). The thirteenth Article of Faith states: "We believe in being honest." These words are so familiar that, for some, they have lost their magnitude. Yet, truth, honesty and integrity are fundamental principles of the gospel, essential to our happiness.

If asked, "Are you honest?" most people would probably answer "Yes." What if the question was more specific: "Have you ever taken a pen or pencil that did not belong to you? Have you ever made personal copies on your employer's copy machine without obtaining permission? Have you ever broken the speed limit? Have you ever cheated on a test? Have you ever lied to get out of doing something? Have you ever eaten a grape or other food item in the grocery store without paying for it? Have you ever made a personal long distance telephone call on your employer's phone? Have you ever lied about your child's age to avoid paying adult prices for movies or airline tickets? Do you honor your commitments by doing what you say you will do?" Could you still claim to be honest in all your dealings?

There are no degrees of honesty. Speaking of this truth, President Howard W. Hunter taught: "There are some who will admit it is morally wrong to be dishonest in big things yet believe it is excusable if those things are of lesser importance. Is there really any difference between dishonesty involving a thousand dollars or that which involves only a dime? Is there any difference in principle between a little white lie and the perjury of a witness in a court of law or before a congressional investigation committee under oath? Are there really degrees of dishonesty, depending upon whether or not the subject is great or small?"[1]

President Spencer W. Kimball said: "Those who take little things without accounting for them, such as fruit from the neighbor's yard, a pen from a desk, a package of gum from the help-yourself shelf, all are being taught silently that little thefts and dishonesties are not so bad."[2]

And from President Gordon B. Hinckley: "We cannot be less than honest, we cannot be less than true, we cannot be less than virtuous if we are to keep sacred the trust given us by those who have gone before us, or if we are to merit the trust and confidence of those with whom we live, work, and associate. Once it was said among our people that a man's word was as good as his bond. Shall any of us be less reliable, less honest than our forebears? Those who are dishonest with others canker their own souls and soon learn that they cannot trust even themselves."[3]

Are you satisfied with your personal standard of truth, honesty and integrity?

1. Howard W. Hunter, "Basic Concepts of Honesty," *New Era*, February 1978, 4.
2. Spencer W. Kimball, edited by Edward L. Kimball, *The Teachings of Spencer W. Kimball*, (Salt Lake City: Bookcraft, 1982), 343.
3. Gordon B. Hinckley, *Stand a Little Taller*, (Salt Lake City: Eagle Gate, 2001), 361.

Truth, Honesty and Integrity

Dares to Improve Your Life

- For a week, I dare you not to lie or exaggerate the truth.
- I dare you to list how dishonesty has affected your relationships with God, family and friends.
- I dare you to consult the Holy Ghost to see if you are being completely honest—trust the promptings.
- I dare you to select one area of your life to become perfectly honest: never take a pen, pencil or anything that does not belong to you; put in an honest day's work; never cheat on a test; obey the laws of the land.

Truth is within each of us. Blaise Pascal must have understood this when he wrote: "We know truth, not only by reason but also by the heart."

As if written in genetic code, truth is a basic part of our divine make-up, something we were endowed with from our Heavenly Father. He has promised us, "by the power of the Holy Ghost ye may know the truth of all things" (Moroni 10:5). Part of our mortal test is to remain true to the truth. It is having the integrity to make our actions consistent with our beliefs. It is having the courage to do what is right, even when no one is watching. It is being true to our divine nature. William Shakespeare penned these familiar lines about truth, honesty and integrity: "To thine own self be true; and it must follow as the night the day, thou canst not then be false to any man."[1]

"Be honest with yourself, others, and the Lord. When you are honest in every way, you build strength of character that will allow you to be of great service to God and others. You will be blessed with peace of mind and self-respect. When you are honest, you will be

---

1. William Shakespeare, Hamlet 1.iii.78-81.

trusted by the Lord and by those around you. Dishonesty hurts you and usually hurts others as well. When you lie, steal, shoplift, or cheat, you damage your spirit and become less able to do good things. Be honest in your job, giving a full amount of work for your pay. Don't rationalize that wrong is right, even though many people around you may think there is no harm in being dishonest. Being honest requires courage and commitment to do what you know is right."[2]

The Lord said: "Thou shalt not steal. Thou shalt not bear false witness" (Exodus 20:15-16). We must not try to rationalize that wrong is right. Elder Joseph B. Wirthlin has said: "The standard by which we should measure our integrity is not the world's standard, but the standard the Lord has given us. Integrity is many things. It is giving an honest day's work to our employer. Integrity is honesty in what we say or imply, avoiding such business practices as misrepresenting ourselves or our products. Integrity implies faithfulness in marriage and family relationships. It means being loyal and true with each other and, most importantly, with ourselves and our Heavenly Father. I know of no way to make our lights shine brighter than by having complete integrity at all times with everyone."[3]

Practice honesty daily, by starting with one area of your life and building on those successes. Do what you say you will do. Be dependable. Never take anything that does not belong to you. Return what you borrow. Keep your promises. Never cheat. Never tell white lies or half-truths. Put in an honest day's work for each day you are paid. Be on time. Honor the laws of the land. Never allow anyone to persuade you to do something you know is wrong.

The English poet Alexander Pope wrote, "Where there is honesty, other virtues will follow."

Do you measure your integrity by the world's standard, or God's standard?

---

2. *For The Strength of Youth, Fulfilling Our Duty to God* pamphlet, The Church of Jesus Christ of Latter-day Saints, 2001, 31.
3. Joseph B. Wirthlin, *Finding Peace in Our Lives* (Salt Lake City: Deseret Book Co., 1995), 79.

Chapter 9

An Attitude of Gratitude

Your Personal Truth

- How does it feel to be unappreciated?
- How often do you humbly and prayerfully thank Heavenly Father for your life and countless other blessings?
- How many minutes—or seconds—did you spend today thanking God for the numerous blessings He has given you?
- Have you ever offered a prayer of thanks—no requests, just expressions of gratitude?

Imagine if you gave your time and resources to another and the recipient offered little or no acknowledgement of your kindness. Our loving Heavenly Father has given us all things, including life itself. How must He feel when we fail to recognize His countless blessings and thank Him for His generosity?

President Joseph F. Smith believed "that one of the greatest sins of which the inhabitants of the earth are guilty today is the sin of ingratitude . . . We see a man raised up with extraordinary gifts, or with great intelligence, and he is instrumental in developing some great principle. He and the world ascribe this great genius and wisdom to himself. He attributes his success to his own energies, labor and mental capacity. He does not acknowledge the hand of God in anything connected with his success, but ignores him altogether and takes the honor to himself . . . In all great modern discoveries in science, in the arts, in mechanics, and in all material advancement of the age, the world says, 'We have done it.' The individual says, 'I have done it,' and he gives no honor or credit to God."[1]

---

1. Joseph F. Smith, *Gospel Doctrine: Selections from the Sermons and Writings of Joseph F. Smith,* compiled by John A. Widtsoe (Salt Lake City: Deseret Book Co., 1939), 270.

Humble recognition of God's blessings brings us closer to Him and increases our faith and happiness. Jesus Christ set the perfect example of humility and gratitude toward our Father in Heaven. Preparing to feed the multitude of four thousand, ". . . he took the seven loaves and the fishes, and gave thanks . . ." (Matt. 15:36). Before raising Lazarus from the dead, ". . . Jesus lifted up his eyes, and said, Father, I thank thee that thou hast heard me" (John 11:41), and seated with His apostles at the Last Supper, knowing the drink represented the shedding of His own blood, ". . . he took the cup, and gave thanks . . ." (Matt. 26:27). In all things, the Savior praised Heavenly Father.

The acknowledgment of blessings has a positive effect on our disposition. David recognized the Lord's hand in his life, to which he joyfully sang, "To the end that my soul may give glory to thy name, and sing praise to thee, and not be silent. O Lord my God, I will give thanks unto thee forever" (*JST* Psalms 30:12).

In a revelation to Joseph Smith, the Lord said: "And he who receiveth all things with thankfulness shall be made glorious; and the things of this earth shall be added unto him, even an hundred fold, yea, more" (D&C 78:19). If we are grateful recipients of His gifts, He will give us more!

Are you a grateful recipient of God's blessings?

An Attitude of Gratitude

Dares to Improve Your Life

- I dare you to time your prayers to discover how many minutes, or seconds, you spend thanking God, and set a goal to increase your performance.

- I dare you to write down 100 things you are grateful for and to acknowledge these gifts from God in your next prayer. I dare you to repeat this challenge again, and again.

- I dare you to offer a prayer to God that is all about Him and the things He has done for you, and not mention anything you want or need.

- For the next 30 days, I dare you to make time each day, in addition to your regular prayers, to humbly acknowledge Heavenly Father's numerous gifts.

Elder Richard L. Evans has said we should "Thank God for all this: for life and what sustains it, for loved ones that make it meaningful, for faith and purpose and continuance, always and forever. Thank God for all of this—and much, much more."[1]

In Luke, we read of ten lepers who cried out to Jesus for mercy. After He healed these men of this horrible disease, only ". . . one of them, when he saw that he was healed, turned back, and with a loud voice glorified God, And fell down on his face at His feet, giving Him thanks . . ." for this magnificent blessing. "And Jesus answering said, Were there not ten cleansed? but where are the nine?" (Luke 17:11-19). Only one turned his heart and soul toward the Savior and praised God for the blessing received. Perhaps the others had busy lives to return to and could not make time to offer a simple "thank you."

---

1. Richard L. Evans, "Thanks: for the Organization and Operation of the Earth," *Improvement Era*, February 1968, 74.

It is easy to reflect on the lepers' situation and believe we would never be remiss in expressing our gratitude. Each day, we should ask ourselves if we are numbered with the one who "glorified God" or with the ungrateful nine?

Recorded in the Book of Mormon, Amulek gave a powerful address to the Zoramites in which he urged, "humble yourselves even to the dust, and worship God, in whatsoever place ye may be in, in spirit and in truth; and that ye live in thanksgiving daily, for the many mercies and blessings which he doth bestow upon you" (Alma 34:38). What sage advice for a joyous life: "live in thanksgiving daily."

In revelation given to the prophet Joseph Smith in this dispensation we are commanded: ". . . Thou shalt love the Lord thy God with all thy heart, with all thy might, mind, and strength . . . [and] Thou shalt thank the Lord thy God in all things" (D&C 59:5, 7).

We express our love for Heavenly Father when we humbly acknowledge His hand in our lives and joyfully thank Him for blessings unnumbered. In the words of David, "Let us come before his presence with thanksgiving, and make a joyful noise unto him with psalms" (Psalms 95:2).

Have you made a joyful noise to the Lord today?

Chapter 10

A Friend of The Savior

> ## Your Personal Truth
>
> - What do you know about Christ?
> - Is it possible to be a friend of Jesus Christ?
> - What price are you willing to pay to have a personal relationship with the Savior?
> - If a friend is one who summons us to do our best, then is Jesus Christ your best friend?

The story is told of a man who died and was resurrected, and waited in a room to be interviewed. The man waiting ahead of him was ushered into the next room and the interviewer began: "I want you to tell me what you know about Jesus Christ." The man responded, "Well, He was born of Mary in Bethlehem; He lived thirty-three years, spending the last three organizing His church, choosing His Apostles, and giving the gospel to direct our lives. He suffered and died so that we could have eternal life. Three days later He was resurrected so that we might return to Heavenly Father." The interviewer interrupted: "Yes, yes, that's all true, but what do you know about Christ." The man, a little perplexed, again began: "Well, He restored the gospel in its fulness to the earth through Joseph Smith." The interviewer again stopped the man saying, "All of what you have said to me is true," then invited the next man into the room. As this man entered, he fell upon his knees before the interviewer and cried, "My Lord, my God."

The Savior declared: "This is life eternal, that they might know . . . Jesus Christ" (John 17:3). Notice that the scripture does not say that we should know some things *about* Him, but that we should *know* Him.

It is critical that we come to "know" Jesus Christ if we are to achieve eternal life. "His is a beckoning friendship," explained Neal A. Maxwell, "a designation that is actually an invitation, for he declared: 'I will call you friends, for ye are my friends, and ye shall have an inheritance with me.'"

A true friend is someone you know well and respect, a person you are interested in and with whom you share your thoughts and feelings, someone who inspires you to better yourself, a person you listen to— an ally.

How do we become a friend to Jesus Christ? That seems an awesome question to consider. The Savior himself has told us how we qualify as His friend: "Ye are my friends, if ye do whatsoever I command you" (John 15:13). And, as a good friend, He has set a perfect example for us to follow.

President Gordon B. Hinckley counseled, "You will find your greatest example in the Son of God. I hope that each of you will make Him your friend. I hope you will strive to walk in His paths, extending mercy, blessing those who struggle, living with less selfishness, reaching out to others."[1]

To prove we are worthy friends of Jesus Christ, we must strive to obey and follow His example. Our friendship is strengthened through prayer, meditation and scripture study of His life and ministry. President Harold B. Lee wrote: "I was preparing myself for a radio talk on the life of the Savior, when I read again the story of the life, the crucifixion, and the resurrection of the Master. There came to me as I read that, a reality of that story. More than just what was on the written page. For in truth, I found myself viewing the scenes with a certainty as though I had been there in person. I know that these things come from the revelation of the living God."[2]

Is your friendship with Jesus Christ close enough that you would recognize Him?

---

1. Gordon B. Hinckley, "The Quest for Excellence," *Ensign,* September 1999, 2.
2. Harold B. Lee, "Divine Revelation," *Speeches of the Year,* Brigham Young University, October 15, 1952, 10.

A Friend of the Savior

Dares to Improve Your Life

- For a month, or longer, I dare you to study the scriptures, looking for clues about the character of Jesus Christ.
- When making important decisions this week, I dare you to start by asking yourself "What would the Savior do?"
- I dare you to read the testimonies of ancient and modern-day prophets, searching for what they have said about Jesus Christ.
- For a month, or longer, I dare you to express your gratitude for the Savior's sacrifice in your daily prayers.

One night a man dreamed he was walking along the beach with the Lord. As scenes of his life flashed before him, he noticed that there were two sets of footsteps in the sand. He also noticed at his saddest, lowest times there was but one set of footsteps. This bothered the man. He asked the Lord, "Did you not promise that if I gave my heart to you that you'd be with me all the way? Then why is there but one set of footprints during my most troublesome times?" The Lord replied, "My precious child, I love you and I would never forsake you. During those times of trial and suffering, when you see only one set of footprints, it was then I carried you."[1]

The Savior knows each of us personally. Because of His atoning sacrifice, He knows us better than we know ourselves. He has an intimate understanding of our pain, suffering, temptations and other challenges (see Alma 7:11-13). There is nothing He cannot comprehend (see D&C 38:2). He not only knows us, but He loves us and wants to helps us (see Alma 36:3; Isaiah 61:1-3). It is vital to the success of our mission in mortality that we gain a personal relationship with Jesus Christ.

---

1. Author unknown.

When the resurrected Savior visited the Nephites, He invited them to "Arise and come forth unto me, that ye may thrust your hands into my side, and also that ye may feel the prints of the nails in my hands and in my feet, that ye may know that I am the God of Israel, and the God of the whole earth, and have been slain for the sins of the world . . . the multitude went forth, and thrust their hands into his side, and did feel the prints of the nails in his hands and in his feet; and this they did do," we read, "going forth one by one" (3 Nephi 11:14, 15). He wanted them to make the relationship personal—to feel for themselves. Similarly, we are each individually responsible for learning about Jesus Christ and making our connection to Him personal.

The time to do it is now—lest we be left outside the wedding feast, like the unwise virgins, who when they pleaded, "Lord, Lord, open unto us," the Bridegroom responded, "Verily, I say unto you, I know you not" (see Matthew 25:1-12). It is interesting to note, that in the prophet Joseph Smith's inspired translation of this passage there is a profound distinction: "But he answered and said, verily I say unto you, *ye know me not*" (JST; Matthew 25:10-11, italics added).

Through His atoning sacrifice, Jesus Christ paid the price to know us and to know how to help us. He wants to help us make it safely home—but He waits for us to request His help: "Behold, I stand at the door and knock: if any man hear my voice, and open the door, I will come in to him, and will sup with him, and he with me" (Revelation 3:20). We must want to make our connection personal, for He has said, "Draw near unto me and I will draw near unto you; seek me diligently and ye shall find me; ask, and ye shall receive; knock, and it shall be opened unto you" (D&C 88:62-63).

Do you have a personal relationship with Jesus Christ?

Chapter 11

Word Power

Your Personal Truth

- Have your words caused another person to feel hurt or embarrassed?
- Do you make negative comments and counter them by saying, "I was only joking"?
- Do your words uplift and inspire your family, friends, neighbors, strangers, and all you come in contact with?
- When you speak unkind words, how does it make your spirit feel afterward?

"Sticks and stones may break my bones, but words will never hurt me," is a childhood rhyme that propagates the myth that words are unimportant and cannot hurt us. But the verse is incorrect. Cruel words can inflict pain and suffering to the same extent that kind and loving words can lift the spirit and warm the heart.

Words lodge in the soul and have an effect on the spirit. They can inspire or they can destroy. Negative words are like the toxic element arsenic: the slow poisoning effect from chronic exposure may go undetected at first, but over time they destroy the spirit—of both the recipient and the tormentor.

It is impossible to imagine the suffering our Savior endured because of cruel words, particularly from those close to Him. Although Jesus foretold that Peter would deny Him, it still must have caused Him great pain when His apostle uttered the words, "I know him not" (Luke 22:57).

Peter experienced the sorrow that comes from being the inflicter of those wounding words, and he also came to know what it felt like to have others speak of him unjustly. He later counseled the Saints to "[lay] aside all malice, and all guile, and hypocrisies, . . . and all evil speakings" (1 Peter 2:1).

Notice Peter did not say it was okay if the person deserves it, or if we feel justified. He said to lay aside "all evil speaking."

Christ's gospel is positive—negative comments support the Adversary in his work to destroy. When choosing our words, President Gordon B. Hinckley urged us to choose the Savior as our role model: "I know that the Lord is pleased when we use clean and virtuous language, for He has set an example for us. His revelations are couched in words that are affirmative, that are uplifting, that encourage us to do what is right and to go forward in truth and goodness."[1]

The wise author of Proverbs wrote: "A soft answer turneth away wrath: but grievous words stir up anger . . . A wholesome tongue is a tree of life: but perverseness therein is a breach in the spirit" (Proverbs 15:1, 4).

Do your words break and destroy the spirit, or nurture and strengthen it?

---

1. Gordon B. Hinckley, "Take Not the Name of God in Vain," *Ensign,* November 1987, 44.

Word Power

Dares to Improve Your Life

- I dare you to accept full responsibility for words you have spoken that have caused another person hurt or embarrassment, and sincerely tell them you are sorry.

- I dare you to pray to become more aware of negative comments when they first come into your mind, before you have spoken them. I dare you to work to eliminate them from your thoughts.

- For today, I dare you to avoid faultfinding and criticizing of other people.

- For today, I dare you to speak only positive comments. Later, record in your journal how it made you feel.

Faultfinding, character assassination and cruel comments are damaging to both the recipient and the purveyor. Too quickly the speaking of negative remarks becomes a rancorous habit that is difficult to break. It is much easier to stop before we say the words.

To help us become more selective of the words we speak, Elder Neal A. Maxwell suggests: "A wise pause can help us to ripen our later comments and keep us from uttering words we would gladly recall later on."[1] Do you remember the sage advice: "When angry, count to ten before speaking"?

Much pain could be avoided if we paused and considered our words before speaking them.

In an epistle to the Ephesians the apostle Paul wrote: "Let no corrupt communication proceed out of your mouth, but that which is good to the use of edifying, that it may minister grace unto the

---

1. Neal A. Maxwell, *That Ye May Believe* (Salt Lake City: Bookcraft, 1992), 132.

hearers. . . . Let all bitterness, and wrath, and anger, and clamour, and evil speaking, be put away from you, with all malice: And be ye kind one to another, tenderhearted, forgiving one another, even as God for Christ's sake hath forgiven you" (Ephesians 4:29, 31-32).

The words "I'm sorry" are often left unsaid because they are difficult to articulate. However, these two simple words, when spoken sincerely, possess the power to miraculously heal wounds and repair broken hearts of both the receiver and the giver of the apology.

Apology is an action word; we ask forgiveness, making amends whenever possible, and promise never to repeat the offense. It is by our future actions to replace all evil speaking with kindness and love that we prove we have repented of the offense. The key is to avoid negative words and strive to eliminate them from our vocabulary. "When at length we tire of putting people down," Elder Maxwell has said, "this self-inflicted fatigue can give way to the invigorating calisthenics of lifting people up."[2]

In the hymn "Nay, Speak No Ill" we sing:

> Nay, speak no ill; a kindly word
> Can never leave a sting behind;
> And, oh, to breathe each tale we've heard
> Is far beneath a noble mind.[3]

Words speak volumes about the character of the person using them.

What do your words say about you?

---

2. Neal A. Maxwell, *Men and Women of Christ* (Salt Lake City: Bookcraft, 1991), 28.

3. *Hymns of The Church of Jesus Christ of Latter-Day Saints,* (Salt Lake City: The Church of Jesus Christ of Latter-day Saints, 1985), no. 233.

Chapter 12

Living With No Regrets

┌───┐

Your Personal Truth

- Are you satisfied with the life you are presently living?
- If you knew you had only 24 more hours to live, who would you want to talk to before you died, and what would you want to tell them?
- Have you put your life on hold until after you graduate, get married, earn a better income, have children, retire?
- How would you change your life if you had only one week left in mortality?

└───┘

The comedian Joe E. Lewis said: "You only live once, but if you work it right, once is enough."

Latter-day Saints know that our time in mortality is a gift from God that can only be used once. To make the most of it, we must live more intensely, more vibrantly, more meaningfully and more purposefully. Each day is a new opportunity to do better. To be more spiritual. To be more faithful. To be more compassionate. To be more creative. To be inspirational. To be loving. To be loved. To laugh more and cry less. To live with gusto!

Too many people get caught in the "as soon as" trap and delay living the life they dream of—the one Heavenly Father wants them to experience. Tragically, they tell themselves: "As soon as I graduate and am living on my own; As soon as I have a more prestigious job; As soon as I lose ten pounds; As soon as I'm married; As soon as I'm older; As soon as I get a new car; As soon as I get physically fit; As soon as we have a house; As soon as our children are grown; As soon as I retire—then I'll have time and energy to really enjoy my life!

The tragedy of this mindset is that even if they do achieve their goal, they have squandered the journey. After all, "It is not the

years in your life, but the life in your years that counts," wrote
Adlai Stevenson.

No one knows how much time they are allotted in mortality. Eck-
hart Tolle astutely wrote, "Realize deeply that the present moment is
all you ever have." We cannot put off laughing, loving and living life
to the fullest until a time in the future that may never come. President
Gordon B. Hinckley has said, "The future—you can anticipate it, but
you can't necessarily do very much about it. It is the present you have
to deal with. Reach out for every good opportunity that you have to
do what you ought to do."[1]

Regardless of circumstances, you ultimately decide if you will live
a life of random existence or one that is potent and dynamic. To the
Thessalonians, Paul wrote, "Rejoice evermore" (1 Thessalonians
5:16). Imagine a day filled with rejoicing: time spent in engaging
conversation with family and friends, going barefoot, watching sun-
sets, climbing trees, reading aloud, singing, dancing, giggling, hold-
ing hands with those you love; experiencing the moment.

Danny Kaye said, "Life is a big canvas, and you should throw all
the paint on it you can."

Will you leave your canvas empty, or paint it with beautiful colors?

---

1. Gordon B. Hinckley, *Interview with Deseret News,* 25 February 2000.

Living With No Regrets

Dares to Improve Your Life

- I dare you to telephone, write, or visit your family and friends and share the words you would want to leave them with if you had only 24 hours to live.

- I dare you to stop putting your life on hold until you graduate, lose weight, get a better job, move into a new house, earn more money, finish raising your children, or whatever your excuse is.

- I dare you to do one thing this week that you've been putting off until things are "better."

- I dare you to make an inventory of your regrets and pray to resolve them.

"Life is action and passion," wrote Oliver Wendell Holmes, Jr., "therefore it is required of a man that he should share the passion and action of time, at peril of being judged not to have lived."

It has been said that the purpose of life is more life. Speaking of the gift of eternal life, the Savior declared, "I am come that they might have life, and that they might have it more abundantly" (John 10:10). Abundant means "fully, amply, in great quantity."[1]

Part of our mortal challenge is to live life more fully, more amply, in great quantity—in short, more abundantly! We need to stop planning for a better life and start experiencing it.

Too often we underestimate our ability to affect our situation in life and delay daily joy. Elder M. Russell Ballard realized this and taught: "We must learn to become creators of circumstances and not creatures of them."[2]

---

1. *An American Dictionary of the English Language*, Noah Webster, 1828.
2. M. Russell Ballard, "Do Things That Make a Difference," *Ensign*, June 1983, 68.

Start today—do something you have been putting off or dreaming about that would make your life richer. Start a journal, put up a basketball hoop, take a swimming class, learn to juggle, write a thank you note, eat ice cream, jump rope, bake cookies for neighbors, clean out the garage, read a book, write a poem, frame some photographs, gather wildflowers, build a snowman, telephone a friend you've lost touch with, express your love to family and friends.

Elder Ballard suggests: "Write down one thing that you are going to start doing that you have been meaning to do for a long time but that you just haven't gotten around to. I don't know what it might be, but place into your life, beginning tonight, one thing that you are going to do that is going to make you a better person."[3]

Memorize the words: "If not now, when?" and ask them of yourself daily.

"It's only when we truly know and understand that we have a limited time on earth—and that we have no way of knowing when our time is up—that we will begin to live each day to the fullest, as if it [were] the only one we had," Elizabeth Kubler-Ross profoundly stated.

A father rushed about, videotaping his daughter's sixth birthday party so that he could enjoy it later. Afterward, he discovered the camera didn't work. In his zeal to record the event, he missed the actual party and now had no videotape to replay it. It was a "life doesn't get any better than this" moment that will never happen again.

"The tragedy of life is not so much what men suffer," wrote Thomas Carlyle, "but rather what they miss."

Did you celebrate today and live with no regrets?

---

3. *Ibid.*

Chapter 13

Rise to the Call

┌───┐

Your Personal Truth

- How faithful are you about performing your church duties and responsibilities?
- How often do you seek the Lord's help in fulfilling your church callings?
- What have you done to support the individuals under your charge and those that you report to?
- What could you do to expand your church service?

└───┘

mag-ni-fy (verb) 1. To make great, or greater; to increase the dimensions of; to amplify; to enlarge, either in fact or in appearance. 2. To increase the importance of; to augment the esteem or respect in which one is held. 3. To praise highly; to laud; to extol.[1]

"Magnify your calling" is an exhortation often heard amongst Latter-day Saints. But what does that really mean?

Based upon the Webster's Dictionary definition, to magnify a position one must enlarge, respect and praise it. Therefore, we magnify our church callings when we respect and esteem the office to which we have been called; focusing our attention on the duties assigned to us and striving to not only do all that is required, but to look for ways to expand our service. We must also support individuals under our charge and those that we report to.

On the topic of callings, President Ezra Taft Benson said, "The Lord expects each of us to have a calling in His church so that others may be blessed by our talents and influence. He expects us to magnify those callings. The way we do that is to do the work which

_____

1. *Webster's Revised Unabridged Dictionary,* 1998.

goes with the calling or the office we accept. Is there a priesthood holder who has not time to visit three, four, five families at least once each month? Is there a sister who is so busy she cannot visit teach? If we are 'too busy' to hold a church calling, we had better look at our priorities."[2]

Have you ever failed to fulfill the duties of your office because you felt unqualified, incapable, discouraged, or that you did not have enough time? We may not be the most capable person called to fill a position, but we are the right person; chosen by God through His called and ordained servants. And, He wants us to succeed. If we humbly ask for His help and exercise faith, through His grace we will receive power to overcome all obstacles before us.

Moroni records the Lord's promise to us: "And if men [and women] come unto me I will show unto them their weakness. I give unto men weakness that they may be humble; and my grace is sufficient for all men that humble themselves before me; for if they humble themselves before me, and have faith in me, then will I make weak things become strong unto them" (Ether 12:27).

With the Lord's help, we can accomplish all that is required and more.

The question is: Do you possess the humility and faith necessary to magnify your Church calling?

2. President Ezra Taft Benson, "Lord, Increase Our Faith," Provo Utah Tabernacle Rededication, 21 September 1986.

Rise to the Call

Dares to Improve Your Life

- I dare you to make a list of the duties and responsibilities of your calling. Then make a second list of work you accomplished in the past week or month toward magnifying your calling. Compare the two lists and identify areas that need improvement.

- I dare you to pray for inspiration to discover ways you can better fulfill the responsibilities of your calling. Write down the ideas and impressions you receive, then work to implement them.

- I dare you to make a list of factors that keep you from magnifying your calling, such as time, other people, fear, and lack of training. Pray for inspiration, ask church leaders for help, and work toward solutions to overcome these stumbling blocks.

- I dare you to make a list of ways you can motivate the individuals that report to you, and help those you report to, to magnify their callings. Do at least one thing on your list this week.

If we "Remember the worth of souls is great in the sight of God" (D&C 18:10), then we must also believe that a calling to serve those whom the Lord so esteems must have great significance and consequence.

After Jacob and Joseph were ordained priests and teachers by their brother Nephi, Jacob tells us that "We did magnify our office unto the Lord, taking upon us the responsibility, answering the sins of the people upon our own heads if we did not teach them the word of God with all diligence; wherefore, by laboring with our might their blood might not come upon our garments; otherwise their blood would come upon our garments, and we would not be found spotless at the last day" (Jacob 1:19).

In this dispensation President John Taylor warned: "If you do not magnify your callings, God will hold you responsible for those you might have saved, had you done your duty."[1]

And Elder Hugh B. Brown gave this charge: ". . . if any of us fail to teach, lead, direct, and help to save those under our direction and within our jurisdiction, then the Lord will hold us responsible if they are lost as the result of our failure."[2]

Are we guilty of sins of omission in fulfilling our Church callings? Is there an inactive or new member who needs fellowshipping? Is there an active member in distress? Are we earnestly teaching the gospel to those under our charge? Do we turn in our reports on time?

Imagine if each Latter-day Saint focused their energy toward amplifying their responsibilities of Beehive secretary, Teachers Quorum counselor, single adults activity leader, visiting teacher, home teacher, chorister, Scoutmaster, Sunday School teacher, enrichment leader, missionary, and church member, in an effort to build up God's kingdom and bring praise to His name. What a difference it would make in the Church, and in the world at large, if each member amplified his or her calling. What better cause is there to be "anxiously engaged in" (D&C 58:27) than that of serving others in Christ's name and under His direction?

The Psalmist David sang, "O magnify the Lord with me, and let us exalt his name together." (Psalms 34:3). Ultimately, when we are called to serve in Christ's Church, it is a call to serve Him. When we magnify our calling, it demonstrates our love and respect for Him. Through our humble service, we laud and extol His name and bring praise to His great work.

Would the Savior be pleased with the quality of your service?

---

1. Quoted by Hugh B. Brown, *Conference Report,* October 1962, 84.
2. Hugh B. Brown, *Conference Report,* October 1962, 84.

Chapter 14

Feast on the Scriptures

Your Personal Truth

- If your scriptures were taken from you for a few weeks, would you really miss them?
- Are you suffering from spiritual starvation and dehydration?
- Does reading the scriptures daily feed your spirit?
- Have you grown to love the scriptures?

Most of us have never felt the dire affects of starvation and dehydration. When our bodies crave nourishment, we feed them. Thirst is quenched with a drink. Yet many are afflicted with spiritual anorexia—their spirits crave the nourishment that can only be fed by the scriptures. Amos prophesied: "Behold, the days come, saith the Lord God, that I will send a famine in the land, not a famine of bread, nor a thirst for water, but of hearing the words of the Lord" (Amos 8:11).

The scriptural famine Amos speaks of no longer exists. There is sustenance available to all who will partake. Latter-day Saints are blessed to have four Gospels, which are the testimony of the Savior's ministry, and the words of living prophets to feast upon. But like the manna given to Moses and the children of Israel that had to be gathered daily (see Exodus 16:15-21), we must feast upon the scriptures each day.

Speaking of spiritual nourishment, President Ezra Taft Benson said, "'Feast upon the words of Christ' (2 Nephi 32:3) by consistently studying the scriptures every day and by following the counsel of the living prophets. Particularly make the study of the Book of Mormon a lifetime pursuit and daily sup from its pages."[1]

---

1. Ezra Taft Benson, *Come, Listen to a Prophet's Voice* (Salt Lake City: Deseret Book Co., 1990), 50.

Many have learned to suppress their craving for the sustenance found only in the scriptures. They do not recognize their self-imposed spiritual anorexia. It is not until they suffer complete spiritual starvation and dehydration that they begin to realize their self-imposed famine.

President Spencer W. Kimball once shared this story about spiritual starvation: "During the war in Vietnam, some of our men were taken prisoner and kept in nearly total isolation. Permitted no access to the scriptures, they later told how they hungered for the words of truth, more than for food, more than for freedom itself. What they would have given for a mere fragment of the Bible or Book of Mormon that lay so idly on our shelves! They learned by hard experience something of Nephi's feelings when he said: 'For my soul delighteth in the scriptures, and my heart pondereth them, and writeth them for the learning and the profit of my children. Behold, my soul delighteth in the things of the Lord; and my heart pondereth continually upon the things which I have seen and heard' (2 Nephi 4:15-16)."[2]

Nephi loved the scriptures. You can feel his passion leap from the page when you read his words. We, too, can and must develop the same love for the word of God. President Gordon B. Hinckley has challenged, "I hope that for you [reading of scriptures] will become something far more enjoyable than a duty; that, rather, it will become a love affair with the word of God. I promise you that as you read, your minds will be enlightened and your spirits will be lifted. At first it may seem tedious, but that will change into a wondrous experience with thoughts and words of things divine."[3]

Appropriately, Henry David Thoreau wrote: "How prompt we are to satisfy the hunger and thirst of our bodies; how slow to satisfy the hunger and thirst of our souls!"

Is your spirit hungry for the words of the Lord?

---

2. Spencer W. Kimball, "How Rare a Possession—the Scriptures!" *Ensign,* September 1976, 2.
3. Gordon B. Hinckley, "The Light Within You," *Ensign,* May 1995, 99.

Feast on the Scriptures

Dares to Improve Your Life

- I dare you to read at least one chapter of scripture a day for a year.
- I dare you to pray before you begin your scripture study, asking that your mind and spirit might be prepared to receive the message.
- I dare you to search the scriptures for an answer to a specific question.
- I dare you to read about the Savior's ministry with the intent to know him better.

Each of us agreed to come on this earthly mission with the goal of returning valiantly. We arrived in mortality with temporary amnesia of our former existence, making it sometimes difficult for us to recognize the correct and only pathway that will lead us back to our Heavenly home. A loving Father, who desires our safe return, has given us the scriptures as a map, instruction manual and light to guide us. The Psalmist aptly wrote: "Thy word is a lamp unto my feet, and a light unto my path" (Psalms 119:105).

President Spencer W. Kimball once explained, "We are pilgrims upon this earth, sent here with a mission to perform, a great work to do, for which we need guidance from the Lord. The fact that I was not born in the times of spiritual darkness in which the heavens were silent and the Spirit withdrawn fills my soul with gratitude. Truly, to be without the word of the Lord to direct us is to be as wanderers in a vast desert who can find no familiar landmarks, or in the dense darkness of a cavern with no light to show us the way to escape."[1] We Latter-day Saints have a light to guide us through the darkness.

---

1. Spencer W. Kimball, "How Rare a Possession—the Scriptures!" *Ensign,* September 1976, 2.

Individuals who study the scriptures know who they are, where they came from, why they are here, and where they want to go. The scriptures teach that we are the literal offspring of God, created in His image and likeness (Genesis 1:26-27), with the potential for exaltation (see Acts 17:29; D&C 76:24). The scriptures teach that we are important in God's plan (see Moses 1:39) and that He wants us to successfully navigate through mortality and return to His presence.

In Lehi's dream, recorded in the Book of Mormon, the iron rod that marked the path to the tree of life and protected the travelers from the dangerous river of water is symbolic of the word of God (see 1 Nephi 8). The analogy teaches us that it is crucial to the success of our spiritual journey that we grasp the word of God if we are to return safely.

One woman's New Year's resolution to read the scriptures daily began as a verse a day. Over time, one verse became two or three a day, then a chapter. By the end of the year she finished the Book of Mormon and had gained a love for the book. The following year, she purchased a study guide to augment her re-reading of the Book of Mormon. What began as a commitment to one verse of scripture per day grew into a passion for study.

A couple decided that instead of watching the morning news on television before going to work, they would read the scriptures. By the end of the year they had read the entire standard works.

The scriptures contain crucial information to guide us safely through mortality. Joseph Smith admonished: "Search the scriptures ... when men receive their instruction from Him that made them, they know how He will save them. Then again we say: Search the Scriptures, search the Prophets and learn what portion of them belongs to you and the people of the nineteenth century."[2]

What did you learn from the scriptures today?

---

2. Joseph Smith, *Teachings of the Prophet Joseph Smith,* selected and arranged by Joseph Fielding Smith (Salt Lake City: Deseret Book Co., 1976), 11.

Chapter 15

Follow Me

Your Personal Truth

- Who has helped you most on your journey through life?
- In what ways have others helped you or contributed to your life?
- What have you done today to help other persons on their journey through life?
- Is your life worthy of emulation?

"When embarking on a new and difficult task, we benefit greatly from having a guide or mentor. For example," explains Elder Victor L. Ludlow, "in learning how to rock-climb, an experienced guide is a must. The guide teaches the principles of climbing before we begin the ascent; he leads the way while scaling the cliff, identifying the best handholds and footholds; additionally, he is capable of rescuing us in case of an accident. In short, a strong, qualified guide makes it possible to safely traverse treacherous terrain, resulting in an exciting and safe experience."[1]

Many colleges and universities pair students with mentors working in their field of interest to answer questions and to act as a guide throughout their professional life. This personal contact with an individual who has already traveled the road the student is about to embark down provides inspiration, vision and clarity. The mentor may open doors, make introductions, teach business procedures and etiquette, and build the apprentice's self-confidence.

Mentoring takes place in many settings: athletics, business, medicine, science, entertainment, education, and other professions.

---

1. Victor L. Ludlow, *Principles and Practices of the Restored Gospel* (Salt Lake City: Deseret Book Co., 1992), 198.

Although situations differ, the process is the same: to provide an example that helps and inspires another to succeed.

A loving mentor has an innate understanding of the Lord's declaration that "the worth of souls is great in the sight of God" (D&C 18:10). They recognize potential and guide their protégés to focus their time, talents and energy toward achieving their goal. "A teacher affects eternity;" wrote Henry Brooks Adams, "he can never tell where his influence stops."[2]

Within the Church are many righteous leaders and teachers worthy of emulation. Personal relationships with individuals whose example motivates us to become better people, deeply enrich our lives. Friedrich Jacobi said, "Every great example takes hold of us with authority of a miracle, and says to us, 'If ye had but faith, ye also could do the same things.'"

There is none more worthy of emulation than Jesus Christ. He is our ultimate mentor, our perfect example. When asked, "What manner of men [and women] ought ye to be?" He answered, "Verily I say unto you, even as I am" (3 Nephi 27:27). He is available twenty-four hours a day, to instruct, inspire and guide us to achieve our goals. He, more than anyone, knows our potential and has a personal interest in seeing us succeed.

What have you learned from the Savior that will help you to be a better person today?

---

2. Henry Brooks Adams, *The Education of Henry Adams* (1907), ch. 20.

Follow Me

Dares to Improve Your Life

- I dare you to find a positive role model that you can turn to for advice and encouragement.
- I dare you to find someone that you can help, influence, or mentor. I dare you to become part of a mentoring program or volunteer your time to help another.
- I dare you to become an intern and learn something from another. Or, I dare you to take on an intern that you can instruct.
- I dare you to learn more about the Savior and select one quality or trait of His to emulate.

In Simon, Jesus Christ recognized the potential for greatness. He changed Simon's name to Peter, meaning "a man of rock," foreshadowing the solid testimony Peter would later develop. Challenged to "follow me" (Matthew 4:19), Peter looked upon the Lord as a teacher and mentor. Over time, this man who had once fished the Sea of Galilee became an inspired fisher of men. Peter's transformation did not happen immediately, but over time. He struggled to become a missionary and even denied the Lord three times. But with a perfect example before him and continued mentoring, Peter grew in strength and conviction and was called to be Christ's chief apostle and leader of His Church.

Modeling the example of the Savior, Peter became more like Him. And he, in turn, became a mentor for members of the Church and his fellow apostles. As he had been challenged to follow, Peter subsequently counseled, "[Christ left] us an example, that ye should follow his steps" (1 Peter 2:21).

The Savior also recognized righteous potential in the misguided Saul and confronted him on the road to Damascus. Acknowledging the error of his ways, Saul hearkened to the voice of the Lord and asked, "what wilt thou have me to do?" (Acts 9:6). Jesus instructed him to seek out a disciple named Ananias that lived in Damascus. Ananias was called by the Lord to tutor Saul in the gospel. The guidance of these spiritual mentors brought about Saul's rebirth. He changed his name to Paul and dedicated his life to building up the kingdom of God.

Paul suffered personal trials, persecution and countless hardships, but remained true and faithful. Serving as a role model and mentor to Timothy, Paul wrote, "But thou hast fully known my doctrine, manner of life, purpose, faith, longsuffering, charity, patience . . . but out of them all the Lord [Paul's ultimate mentor] delivered me" (2 Timothy 3:10-11).

There is a Hindu proverb that says, "Help thy brother's boat across, and lo! thine own has reached the shore." The true joy of mentoring is found in the reciprocal process, when the receiver becomes the giver, helping others to achieve their goals. President Brigham Young said Latter-day Saints "have got to learn that the interest of their brethren is their own interest, or they never can be saved in the Celestial Kingdom of God."[1]

The Lord himself declared, "This is my work and my glory—to bring to pass the immortality and eternal life of man" (Moses 1:39). A mentor in the gospel plays a vital role in this glorious cause.

What will you do today to help another achieve success?

---

1. Brigham Young, *Deseret News,* 18 June 1856, 116.

Chapter 16

Financial Freedom

Your Personal Truth

- Do you use credit to finance impulsive purchases and luxuries?
- What value do you place on the peace of mind that comes from being debt free?
- Do you heed the counsel of the Lord and his prophets to be free from debt?
- Have you mortgaged your future?

"Buy now, pay later" is the "Eat, drink, and be merry . . . and it shall be well with us" (2 Nephi 28:7) philosophy of finance. "To buy on the installment plan means to mortgage your future earnings," taught President J. Reuben Clark Jr. "If through sickness or death, or through loss of work, the earnings cease, the property bought is lost together with what has been put into it."[1]

Debt, like sin, is enslaving until we take the necessary steps to free ourselves from its bondage. "Interest never sleeps nor sickens nor dies," said President Clark. "Once in debt, interest is your companion every minute of the day and night; you cannot shun it or slip away from it; you cannot dismiss it; it yields neither to entreaties, demands, or orders; and whenever you get in its way or cross its course or fail to meet its demands, it crushes you."[2]

Credit card companies are master marketers whose goal is to convince us we deserve to have the things we want now, before we have earned them. They aggressively target young adults, offering t-shirts, discount airfares and other incentives for filling out credit applica-

---

1. J. Reuben Clark Jr., *Conference Report,* April 1938, 103.
2. *Ibid.*

tions. Many, they realize, will not be able to avoid the temptation to use a credit card to buy now and pay later. Too quickly, interest charges are incurred and what seemed like a nominal amount to borrow has become a burdensome debt.

We should not heed "the current cries" that "tempt us to compete for ownership of the things of this world," counseled Elder L. Tom Perry. "We think we need a larger home with a three-car garage, a recreational vehicle parked next to it. We long for designer clothes, extra TV sets (all with VCRs), the latest-model computers, and the newest car. We think we must involve our children in costly activities such as athletic camps and similarly expensive programs. Often these items are purchased with borrowed money and without any thought of providing for our future needs. The results of all of this instant gratification are overloaded bankruptcy courts and families that are far too preoccupied with their financial burdens."[3]

The Lord taught, "A good name is rather to be chosen than great riches, and loving favour rather than silver and gold" (Proverbs 22:1). Many have tarnished their good name by incurring debt to live beyond their financial means. A payment is late, then missed, interest rates and penalty fees escalate, and the debtor's once good name is marred by bad credit history—or they flee their obligations altogether through bankruptcy. Some are tempted to perform dishonest acts in an attempt to pay their debts. No matter how small the loan, "the borrower is servant to the lender" (Proverbs 22:7) until the debt is paid.

Elder Perry has said: "A well-managed family does not pay interest—it earns it."[4]

Are you earning interest or incurring it?

---

3. L. Tom Perry, "If Ye Are Prepared Ye Shall Not Fear," *Ensign,* November 1995, 35.
4. *Ibid.*

Financial Freedom

Dares to Improve Your Life

- I dare you to make a list of all your financial obligations and set a plan to become debt free.
- If you do not already have a savings plan, I dare you to begin one, however small, starting with your next paycheck.
- I dare you to determine one financial obligation you can lower or do without—a mobile telephone, extra cable television channels, VHS rentals, manicures, sporting events, concerts, fast food—and use the money you save to pay off your debts.
- I dare you determine a workable budget, write it down, and commit to live within it.

"Pay as you go" was a motto that President Joseph F. Smith believed in and lived by. He often admonished Latter-day Saints "to aim and diligently endeavor to free themselves from debt."[1]

In the scriptures we read the Lord's counsel about financial matters: "pay thy debt, and live" (2 Kings 4:7), "owe no man any thing" (Romans 13:8), "pay the debt thou hast contracted . . . release thyself from bondage" (D&C 19:35), and this practical advice: "For which of you, intending to build a tower, sitteth not down first, and counteth the cost, whether he have sufficient to finish it?" (Luke 14:28). The Lord wants us to be free, and part of freedom is being financially independent.

President Ezra Taft Benson warned: "Many people do not believe that serious recession will ever come again. Feeling secure in their expectations of continuing employment and a steady flow of wages and salaries, they obligate their future income without thought of what they would do if they should lose their jobs or if their income

---

1. Joseph F. Smith, *Conference Report,* October 1903, 97.

were stopped for some other reason. But the best authorities have repeatedly said that we are not yet smart enough to control our economy without downward adjustments. Sooner or later these adjustments will come."[2]

Money management requires wise judgment and self-discipline. First, we must learn to distinguish between a want and a need, and make wise decisions in budgeting and planning our personal finances. Second, "It takes self-discipline to avoid the 'buy now, pay later' philosophy and to adopt the 'save now and buy later' practice,"[3] counseled President James E. Faust.

Like all other commandments, sound financial management also comes with a blessing: "If there is any one thing that will bring peace and contentment into the human heart, and into the family, it is to live within our means," said President Heber J. Grant. "And if there is any one thing that is grinding and discouraging and disheartening, it is to have debts and obligations that one cannot meet."[4]

"Did you ever see anybody who went in debt and mortgaged and bonded that which he possessed, as free, as independent, as happy as the man who paid for what he had as he went along?" President Joseph F. Smith once asked. "We should live according to our means, and lay a foundation upon which we can build, and upon which our children can build after us, without paying interest on bonded debts incurred by us. I am aware that I am not preaching the financial gospel of the world. I suppose I am laying myself open to the charge of being called a mossback, non-progressive, and so on. All of these epithets are hurled at the men that dare to tell the people to live within their means . . ."[5]

Which financial philosophy are you living: "buy now, pay later" or "save now, buy later?"

---

2. Ezra Taft Benson, "Pay Thy Debt, and Live," 3.
3. James E. Faust, "The Responsibility for Welfare Rests with Me and My Family," *Ensign,* May 1986, 20.
4. Heber J. Grant, *Gospel Standards,* comp. G. Homer Durham (1941), 111.
5. Joseph F. Smith, *Deseret Weekly;* 19 August 1893, 283.

Chapter 17

Purpose in Life

Your Personal Truth

- Do you live your daily life deliberately, with a divine intention?
- Do you believe that God reserved you to come to the earth at this time for a specific purpose?
- Have you asked Heavenly Father to help you discover your purpose in life?
- Are you making decisions and setting goals that will help you achieve your purpose in life?

To live meaningfully is to have a definable purpose in life and to approach each day with divine intent. It is living deliberately, unfettered by external influences; knowing who we are and why we are here. It is discovering and utilizing our unique talents and skills to build the kingdom of God.

Jesus Christ set a perfect example of one who came to know His purpose in life and achieved it. Illustrating this truth, Lloyd D. Newell writes: "When Mary found the twelve-year-old Jesus after thinking He was lost somewhere in the streets of Jerusalem, He innocently responded to her questions: 'How is it that ye sought me? wist ye not that I must be about my Father's business?' (Luke 2:49.) Jesus was so sure about His divine inheritance and His unique mission that He was puzzled that His mother would even wonder about His whereabouts. In His mind, He should not have been anywhere else but in the temple, His Father's house."[1]

---

1. Lloyd D. Newell, *The Divine Connection: Understanding Your Inherent Worth* (Salt Lake City: Deseret Book Co., 1992), 41.

But Jesus did not come into mortality with a perfect knowledge of who He was and the great purpose of His life. Like each of us, His eyes were veiled from the knowledge of His pre-existence. President Lorenzo Snow taught, ". . . during His progress it was revealed unto Him who He was, and for what purpose He was in the world. The glory and power He possessed before He came into the world was made known unto Him."[2] Just as the Savior came to know His purpose in life, so may we.

Our private prayers allow us to speak directly with our Heavenly Father. As we humbly kneel before Him, we should ask Him to help us catch a glimpse of who we are and obtain His direction. As the scriptures direct: "every purpose is established by counsel" (Proverbs 20:18). Speaking of divine counsel, Bishop H. Burke Peterson instructed: "If you will let Him, I testify that our Father in Heaven will walk with you through the journey of life and inspire you to know your special purpose here."[3] He did not send us here to waste life on meaningless pursuits. We are among the "choice spirits who were reserved to come forth in the fulness of times to take part in laying the foundations of the great latter-day work" (D&C 138:53).

We each have a responsibility to discover our purpose in life and live each day with that intention in mind. President Gordon B. Hinckley has said: "You can be excellent in every way. You can be first class. There is no need for you to be a scrub. Respect yourself. Do not feel sorry for yourself. Do not dwell on unkind things others may say about you. Polish and refine whatever talents the Lord has given you. Go forward in life with a twinkle in your eye and a smile on your face, with great and strong purpose in your heart. Love life and look for its opportunities, and forever and always be loyal to the Church."[4]

Have you enough faith to discover your purpose in life?

---

2. Lorenzo Snow, *Conference Report,* April 1901, 3.
3. H. Burke Peterson, "Your Life Has a Purpose," *New Era,* May 1979, 4-5.
4. Gordon B. Hinckley, *Stand A Little Taller,* (Salt Lake City: Eagle Gate, 2001), 298.

Purpose in Life

Dares to Improve Your Life

- I dare you to pray each day for a week, to discover your purpose in life.
- I dare you to read your patriarchal blessing and write down specific references to your purpose in life.
- Each day for a week, I dare you to take a few minutes to ponder your purpose in life.
- I dare you to select one aspect of the Savior's life and try to emulate it daily for a month.

Have you ever considered the wonder of handmade pottery? Each unique vessel begins as the common material called clay. Differing organic matter and mineral deposits give clay its individual color, ranging from various shades of white, through gray, tan, orange, brick red, and dark brown. Common clay, in the hands of a master potter, can be molded and shaped into a vessel both unique and purposeful.

Each of us has at some time felt insignificant. The Adversary would have us believe we are common or useless. Not so. The Lord created each of us with differing strengths and weaknesses, likes and dislikes, talents and skills. In the hands of our Master, the Savior Jesus Christ, each of us has been molded and shaped into a person that is both unique and purposeful.

In order for the potter to throw a symmetrical form, he must first coax the clay to the exact center of the bat on his wheel. If the clay is not centered, it cannot be shaped properly and will almost certainly be thrown from the wheel. In order for us to achieve our purpose in life we must become centered on Christ so that we will not be thrown from our eternal course.

Who better to help us discover and fulfill our purpose than He who has created us and walked before us? President Gordon B. Hinckley counseled, "You will find your greatest example in the Son of God. I hope that each of you will make Him your friend. I hope you will strive to walk in His paths, extending mercy, blessing those who struggle, living with less selfishness, reaching out to others."[1] He who invites us to "come follow me" (Matthew 4:19) is committed to help us discover and achieve our purpose in life.

As we strive to emulate the Savior, we become pliable in His hands, so that He can mold and shape us. President Harold B. Lee explained that Jesus Christ is "the greatest of all teachers . . . He has given you and me hands. He has given you and me brains, and he hasn't given them to us to waste. He expects us to lean on him and exercise [our hands and minds] to the best of our ability in order to use them righteously in righteous purposes."[2]

If there is any doubt that the Lord reserved you to come to the earth for a specific purpose, He has promised, "Ask, and it shall be given you; seek, and you shall find; knock, and it shall be opened unto you: For every one that asketh receiveth; and he that seeketh findeth; and to him that knocketh it shall be opened" (Matthew 7:7-8).

If we will turn to the Savior for direction, He will shape us into the purposeful vessels He knows we can become. The prophet Isaiah wrote, ". . . we are the clay, and thou our potter; and we all are the work of thy hand" (Isaiah 64:8).

Do you believe the Master created you to perform a unique purpose?

---

1. Gordon B. Hinckley, "The Quest for Excellence," *Ensign*, September 1999, 2.
2. Harold B. Lee, *The Teachings of Harold B. Lee*, edited by Clyde J. Williams (Salt Lake City: Bookcraft, 1996), 77.

Chapter 18

Words of Wisdom

Your Personal Truth

- Is having a healthy body important to your spiritual growth?
- Do you eat healthy meals and avoid too much junk food?
- Do you get enough exercise to keep your spirit strong and your attitude positive?
- What are some specific things you could do to improve your physical health?

"Do you maintain proper exercise that will give you the extra energy and alertness of mind to keep your spirit strong and your attitude positive? Are you wise in your diet? Do you avoid the unnutritious snacks that might keep your stomach full but your health quite empty?"[1] Do you get enough sleep so that your body is rested and your mind alert? Are you addicted to caffeinated soft drinks? Do you eat meat sparingly? Do you drink enough water to hydrate your body? Do you fully live the Word of Wisdom?

When asked, "Do you live the Word of Wisdom?" most Latter-day Saints would probably answer, "Yes." If pressed, "Do you honestly live the Word of Wisdom fully?" how many might reconsider?

The Word of Wisdom is much more than abstinence from coffee, tea, tobacco and alcohol. It is an inspired instruction manual for good health maintenance and spiritual growth (see D&C 89). A thorough study of its teachings reveals areas where many Latter-day Saints can find opportunity for improvement.

Recognizing the importance of keeping both spiritual and physical health, the First Presidency and Quorum of the Twelve have given

---

1. Joseph B. Wirthlin, "Little Things Count," *New Era*, May 1988, 4.

this instruction: "Nutritious meals, regular exercise, and appropriate sleep are necessary for a strong body, just as consistent scripture study and prayer strengthen the mind and spirit . . . When you observe the Word of Wisdom (see D&C 89) and other good health practices, you remain free and have control over your life. You gain the blessings of an undefiled body, an alert mind, and the ability to receive help and support from your Heavenly Father through the Holy Ghost."[2]

And from President Ezra Taft Benson: "The condition of the physical body can affect the spirit. That is why the Lord gave us the Word of Wisdom. He also said that we should retire to our beds early and arise early (see D&C 88:124), that we should not run faster than we have strength (see D&C 10:4; Mosiah 4:27), and that we should use moderation in all good things. In general, the more food we eat in its natural state and the less it is refined without additives, the healthier it will be for us. Food can affect the mind, and deficiencies in certain elements in the body can promote mental depression. A good physical examination periodically is a safeguard and may spot problems that can be remedied. Rest and physical exercise are essential, and a walk in the fresh air can refresh the spirit."[3]

Around 42 B.C., Publius Syrus astutely wrote: "Good health and good sense are two of life's greatest blessings."

Do you have the good sense to commit to improving your health habits?

---

2. *For the Strength of Youth* pamphlet, The Church of Jesus Christ of Latter-day Saints, 1990, 12.
3. Ezra Taft Benson, *The Teachings of Ezra Taft Benson* (Salt Lake City: Bookcraft, 1988), 475-476.

Words of Wisdom

Dares to Improve Your Life

- I dare you to read and study Doctrine and Covenants section 89—the Word of Wisdom.

- When reading the Word of Wisdom, I dare you to make a list of the commandments and blessings promised.

- For the next week, I dare you to pray for guidance to see ways you can improve in keeping the Word of Wisdom.

- In whatever area you need improvement—exercising, eating more healthily, quitting a habit that violates the Word of Wisdom—I dare you to set a goal to improve and commit to work on it daily for the next month.

Our physical bodies are a necessary part of our eternal progression. They are a gift from God, who has given us stewardship over them. The practice of good physical health is an expression of love—loving ourselves enough to care for our physical bodies and loving our Heavenly Father enough to obey His commandments (see D&C 89 and 88:124).

The apostle Paul understood the divine gift of our physical bodies and wrote: "Know ye not that ye are the temple of God, and that the Spirit of God dwelleth in you? If any man defile the temple of God, him shall God destroy; for the temple of God is holy, which temple ye are" (1 Corinthians 3:16-17).

Our physical health affects every facet of our life—our proficiency to work, our sense of well-being, concentration, aptitude for learning, self-esteem, interaction with others, stamina, feelings of tension and anxiety, our spirituality, our ability to draw nearer to the Lord, and much more. It is so important to the Lord that we care for our physical bodies and obey the Word of Wisdom that He made it a condition of our receiving a temple recommend, and thereby a stipulation for exaltation.

Illustrating this point, President Gordon B. Hinckley once shared: "I recall a bishop's telling me of a woman who came to get a [temple] recommend. When asked if she observed the Word of Wisdom, she said that she occasionally drank a cup of coffee. She said, 'Now, bishop, you're not going to let that keep me from going to the temple, are you?' To which he replied, 'Sister, surely you will not let a cup of coffee stand between you and the house of the Lord'."[1]

When we obey the Word of Wisdom, Heavenly Father has promised us many blessings, including: "wisdom and great treasures of knowledge, even hidden treasures" (D&C 89:19). One of the many treasures we receive is the privilege of going to the temple, where we gain wisdom and the possibility of exaltation.

The challenge is to not become complacent in the care of our physical bodies. Each of us must evaluate our performance and look for ways to improve. Begin a regular program of walking or other exercise. Eat less junk food and more nutritious meals. Quit an additive soft drink habit: "With reference to cola drinks, the Church has never officially taken a position on this matter, but the leaders of the Church have advised, and we do now specifically advise, against the use of any drink containing harmful habit-forming drugs under circumstances that would result in acquiring the habit. Any beverage that contains ingredients harmful to the body should be avoided."[2] Retire earlier so you can get enough sleep and wake refreshed. Get a yearly physical examination. Drink more water, and fewer beverages with no nutritional benefit.

John Farrar wrote, "There is only one real failure in life that is possible, and that is, not to be true to the best one knows."

Do you love your Heavenly Father, and yourself, enough to take care of your physical body?

---

1. Gordon B. Hinckley, "Keeping the Temple Holy," *Ensign,* May 1990, 49.
2. "Policies and Procedures," The Church of Jesus Christ of Latter-day Saints, May 1972, 50.

Chapter 19

Developing Spiritual Traits

Your Personal Truth

- What spiritual trait do you most want to develop further?
- What spiritual quality are you working on today?
- Have you ever prayed for help to develop a spiritual trait?
- What do you consider the most important character trait a person can have?

Each day is an opportunity for us to reinvent ourselves, to develop the spiritual qualities we want to possess. Gabriel Garcia Marquez must have understood this when he wrote: ". . . human beings are not born once and for all on the day their mothers give birth to them, but that life obliges them over and over again to give birth to themselves."[1] Life is not stagnant. We are either actively becoming more of who we want to be or drifting further away from our purpose.

President David O. McKay often mentioned, "Man's earthly existence is but a test as to whether he will concentrate his efforts, his mind, his soul upon things which contribute to the comfort and gratification of his physical nature, or whether he will make as his life's pursuit the acquisition of spiritual qualities."[2]

The scriptures speak of the spiritual traits we should acquire. The Apostle Peter suggested: "giving all diligence, add to your faith virtue; and to virtue knowledge; and to knowledge temperance; and to temperance patience; and to patience godliness; and to godliness brotherly kindness; and to brotherly kindness charity" (2 Peter 1:5-7). In this dispensation, the prophet Joseph Smith wrote: "We believe in

---

1. Gabriel Garcia Marquez, *Love in the Time of Cholera.*
2. Quoted by Thomas S. Monson, "Faces and Attitudes," *New Era,* September 1977, 47.

being honest, true, chaste, benevolent, virtuous, and in doing good to all men" (Articles of Faith 13).

The list may seem daunting, unless we face it one trait at a time, remembering we are literally the offspring of divinity, blessed with the potential for exaltation (see D&C 132:19-20). Elder Joseph B. Wirthlin has said: "As children of our Heavenly Father, we each have within us every potential of character, of compassion, joy, and of knowledge that we need in our quest for personal growth. The seeds for each godly character trait are in each of us. With that assurance, we are truly able to grow toward godhood as He has commanded us."[3] Developing our spiritual traits is not a suggestion; we have been commanded to do so.

It has been said, "If you always do what you always did—you'll always get what you always got." Each day is an opportunity to grow toward godhood. It begins by making a conscious decision to do something. Eugene F. Ware caught the essence of this process when he wrote: "All glory comes from daring to begin." With that in mind, we must select the spiritual trait we want to acquire and begin work today to obtain it.

What spiritual trait are you working on today?

---

3. Joseph B. Wirthlin, "Little Things Count," *New Era,* May 1988, 4.

Developing Spiritual Traits

Dares to Improve Your Life

- For the next 24 hours, I dare you to act as if you already possess the spiritual quality or trait you most want to develop.

- As you try on a spiritual trait for 24 hours, I dare you to write down what it feels like to possess that quality.

- For a month, I dare you to pray daily for God to help you develop the spiritual trait you are working to acquire.

- I dare you to read in the scriptures about the spiritual trait you want to acquire and mark passages you can refer to later.

It is the little things in life that count, that add up to big things. The Lord has said, "Wherefore, be not weary in well-doing, for ye are laying the foundation of a great work. And out of small things proceedeth that which is great" (D&C 64:33). The steps we take, no matter how small, toward developing our spiritual traits are carrying us closer to the person we ultimately want to become. Alma recognized this truth and counseled his son Helaman: "But behold I say unto you, that by small and simple things are great things brought to pass" (Alma 37:6).

In our day, Elder Joseph B. Wirthlin has given this counsel: "I have been impressed recently with the thought that this life is made up of little things—little things that count a great deal. I believe that the little things are of great importance in our relationship with ourselves, in our relationship with others, and in our relationship with God."[1]

Speaking of the many little things that build our spiritual traits, President David O. McKay said: "Every noble impulse, every unselfish expression of love, every brave suffering for the right; every

---

1. Joseph B. Wirthlin, "Little Things Count," *New Era*, May 1988, 4.

surrender of self to something higher than self; every loyalty to an ideal; every unselfish devotion to principle; every helpfulness to humanity; every act of self-control; every fine courage of the soul, undefeated by pretense or policy, but by being, doing, and living of good for the very good's sake—that is spirituality."[2]

An important quality in obtaining and refining our spiritual traits is faith. In D&C 4:6 the first quality we are told to obtain is faith: "Remember faith, virtue, knowledge, temperance, patience, brotherly kindness, godliness, charity, humility, diligence," and in the next verse we are given this instruction: "Ask, and ye shall receive; knock, and it shall be opened unto you" (D&C 4:7). As our faith grows stronger, so does our desire and ability to acquire additional spiritual traits. We have a greater desire to study the scriptures, our prayers become more intense and personal, and we feel closer to our Father in Heaven and Jesus Christ.

As we draw nearer to Heavenly Father and the Savior, we have a greater desire to be like them: humble, kind, charitable, patient, virtuous, diligent, and godly. Each little building of spiritual traits brings its own blessings and with it, the promise that we are becoming like the person we want to be. The lengthy journey toward exaltation is accomplished one little step at a time.

What little step will you take today?

---

2. Quoted in "Something Higher Than Self," *Speeches of the Year*, 12 October 1965, 4-5.

Chapter 20

Blessings of Temple Worship

Your Personal Truth

- Do you sustain the prophet by obeying his instruction to attend the temple often?

- Do you treat lightly the blessing of having so many temples of God on the earth?

- How do you keep the influence of the temple strong in your life?

- When participating in temple ordinances, do you listen intently to the covenants you are making and blessings you are promised?

Temple worship is an essential part of the gospel of Jesus Christ. It is within the walls of these sacred houses of the Lord that we prepare for exaltation in the celestial kingdom. Marriages and families are sealed together for all eternity. Only in the temple can we receive ordinances and make covenants that will qualify us to return to the presence of our Heavenly Father. No wonder we "shouted for joy" (Job 38:7) when the "plan of happiness" (Alma 42:28) was presented in the pre-existence.

The endowment, which is received only in the Lord's temple, is a necessary and sacred ordinance. President Brigham Young taught, "Your endowment is, to receive all those ordinances in the house of the Lord, which are necessary for you, after you have departed this life, to enable you to walk back to the presence of the Father, passing the angels who stand as sentinels, being enabled to give them the key words, the signs and tokens, pertaining to the Holy Priesthood, and gain your eternal exaltation . . ."[1]

---

1. Brigham Young, *Discourses of Brigham Young,* sel. John A. Widtsoe (Salt Lake City: Deseret Book Co., 1941), 416.

Our inspired prophet and leaders have repeatedly urged us to attend the temple often. There is no other place on earth where we can come as close to recapturing the depth of joy we felt in the pre-existent world. The sacred ordinances performed there are manifestations of love: our Heavenly Father and Jesus Christ's love for us, our love for them, love of family, and love of all mankind that has and will ever exist in mortality. Within the temple, that love is "eternally bound in the heavens" (D&C 132:46).

President Gordon B. Hinckley speaks often of his desire for us to attend the temple regularly. More temples have been built under his leadership than that of all other prophets combined. He has said: "I hope that everyone gets to the temple on a regular basis. I hope your children over 12 years of age have the opportunity of going to the temple to be baptized for the dead. If we are a temple-going people, we will be a better people, we will be better fathers and husbands, we will be better wives and mothers. I know your lives are busy. I know that you have much to do. But I make you a promise that if you will go to the house of the Lord, you will be blessed, life will be better for you. Now, please, please, my beloved brethren and sisters, avail yourselves of the great opportunity to go to the Lord's house and thereby partake of all of the marvelous blessings that are yours to be received there."[2]

Are you too busy to enjoy the blessings of temple worship?

---

2. "Excerpts from Recent Addresses of President Gordon B. Hinckley," *Ensign,* July 1997, 72.

89

Blessings of Temple Worship

Dares to Improve Your Life

- I dare you to select a specific day to attend the temple (or to become worthy to do so), mark the date on your calendar, and let nothing stop you from keeping that commitment.

- If you are endowed and live near a temple, I dare you to select a weekly or monthly day to attend the temple and commit to do so. If you live farther away, I dare you to plan a temple trip this year. If you are not yet endowed, I dare you to offer to baby sit for parents, family or friends while they attend the temple.

- The next time you attend the temple, I dare you to go with the intent to learn something new.

- I dare you to organize or participate in a ward temple trip.

The temple is a place of love, a place of peace, a place of revelation, a place of learning, a place of light, a place of sanctuary, and a place of service, where we receive ordinances and make covenants for time and all eternity. We should yearn to go to the temple often, like David who wrote, "One thing I desire of the LORD, that will I seek after; that I may dwell in the house of the LORD all the days of my life, to behold the beauty of the LORD, and to enquire in his temple" (Psalms 27:4) and "I was glad when they said unto me, Let us go into the house of the LORD" (Psalms 122:1).

Each of us is at a different station on the road to eternal life. Whether you have received your endowment or are working toward doing so, each of us, including youth who may perform baptisms for the dead, should strive to be worthy to attend the temple as often as circumstances will allow.

"Every time you go to the temple, you will be a better man or woman when you leave than you were when you came," stated President Gordon B. Hinckley. "I believe that with all my heart. I make you that promise. Redouble your efforts and your faithfulness in going to the temple and the Lord will bless you. You will be happier."[1]

Our spirits yearn for us to learn of and achieve our divine potential. The Savior asked the Nephites, "What manner of men ought ye to be?" Then He answered his own query, "even as I am" (3 Nephi 27:27). Within the walls of the temple we receive instruction to help us become more like Christ—our very service there helps us become more like Him. President Gordon B. Hinckley has said: "Vicarious temple work for the dead more nearly approaches the vicarious sacrifice of the Savior Himself than any other work of which I know. No one comes with any expectation of thanks for the work which he or she does. It is given with love, without hope of compensation, or repayment. What a glorious principle!"[2]

"I urge our people everywhere, with all of the persuasiveness of which I am capable, to live worthy to hold a temple recommend, to secure one and regard it as a precious asset, and to make a greater effort to go to the house of the Lord and partake of the spirit and the blessings to be had therein. I am satisfied that every man or woman who goes to the temple in a spirit of sincerity and faith leaves the house of the Lord a better man or woman. There is need for constant improvement in all of our lives. There is need occasionally to leave the noise and the tumult of the world and step within the walls of a sacred house of God, there to feel His spirit in an environment of holiness and peace."[3]

Does your spirit not long to "dwell in the house of the Lord"?

---

1. Gordon B. Hinckley, *Stand A Little Taller,* (Salt Lake City: Eagle Gate, 2001), 129.
2. *Ibid.,* 25.
3. Gordon B. Hinckley, "Of Missions, Temples, and Stewardship," *Ensign,* November 1995, 51.

Chapter 21

A Theme Song

Have you ever found yourself tapping your fingers or moving your feet to a musical beat? Or had your eyes fill with tears listening to a song? Ever been driving down the road and a song comes on the radio that you find yourself singing along to? Have you ever hummed along to a commercial jingle or to the theme song from a television program?

Music is all around us. We hear it in elevators, at the supermarket, the mall, the gym, doctors' and dentists' offices, at sporting events, and worship services. Music is carefully placed in advertising campaigns, television programs and movies to underscore the words and pictures, and trigger a particular emotional response from the audience. Through music, we can instantly recall memories of special moments and events in our lives.

Music has a powerful effect on our emotions. Leo Tolstoy astutely wrote: "Music is the shorthand of emotion." It can uplift, inspire, gladden, energize, calm, soothe, relax, and promote reverence.

In the Old Testament we read of the power of music to lift one's spirit: "David took a harp, and played with his hand: so Saul was refreshed, and was well, and the evil spirit departed from him" (1 Samuel 16:23). "The Lord, Himself, was prepared for His greatest test through [music's] influence," reminded Elder Boyd K. Packer, "for the scripture records: 'And when they had sung an hymn, they went out into the Mount of Olives' (Mark 14:26)."[1]

Conversely, music can also elicit negative thoughts and feelings. The Lord's standards, outlined in the Church's *For the Strength of Youth* pamphlet and taught by the First Presidency and Quorum of the Twelve, caution that music can be used for wicked purposes: "Unworthy music may seem harmless, but it can have evil effects on your mind and spirit. Choose carefully the music you listen to. Pay attention to how you feel when you are listening. Don't listen to music that drives away the Spirit . . ."[2]

Elder Packer counseled that we should rid ourselves of music that does not uplift. "Keep just the best of it. Be selective in what you consume and what you produce. It becomes part of you."[3]

And from President Ezra Taft Benson: "listen to uplifting music, both popular and classical, that builds the spirit. Learn some favorite hymns . . ."[4]

"Music is an important and powerful part of life." Used properly it can educate, edify, inspire, and unite. "It can be an influence for good that helps [us] draw closer to Heavenly Father."[5] Berthold Auerbach understood the power of music to uplift and inspire when he said: "Music washes away from the soul the dust of everyday life."

Do you have a song that inspires and cleanses your soul?

1. Boyd K. Packer, "Inspiring Music—Worthy Thoughts," *Ensign,* January 1974, 25.
2. *For The Strength of Youth, Fulfilling Our Duty to God* pamphlet, The Church of Jesus Christ of Latter-day Saints, 2001, 20.
3. Boyd K. Packer, "Inspiring Music—Worthy Thoughts," *Ensign,* January 1974, 25.
4. Ezra Taft Benson, "To the Young Women of the Church," *Ensign,* November 1986, 84.
5. *For the Strength of Youth, Fulfilling Our Duty to God* pamphlet, The Church of Jesus Christ of Latter-day Saints, 2001, 20.

A Theme Song

Dares to Improve Your Life

- I dare you to select a song that makes you feel happy and make it your theme song.
- I dare you to memorize the words of a hymn or inspiring song.
- Whenever a negative feeling or impression comes into your thoughts, I dare you to sing aloud, hum or repeat in your mind the words of an inspiring song.
- I dare you to notice the words of hymns, the messages they teach, the spirit they convey, and to sing them in a spirit of praise, love and devotion.

A powerful way to combat negative thoughts and feelings is by having a personal theme song that you sing aloud or in your head. Select a favorite hymn or other song with words that uplift and inspire, and memorize it. Whenever fear or impure thoughts come into your mind, think through the words of your theme song and it will drive the unworthy impressions away. No special musical ability is required to think a song. Eventually, it will become a habit and you will discover your mind automatically turns on your theme song whenever a negative influence tries to enter your thoughts.

Elder Boyd K. Packer has spoken of the power of having a personal theme song. "In due time you will find yourself, on occasion, humming the music inwardly. As you retrace your thoughts, you discover some influence from the world about you encouraged an unworthy thought to move on stage in your mind, and the music almost automatically began."[1]

---

1. Boyd K. Packer, *Conference Report,* October 1973, 24-25.

Heavenly Father knows the power of music to uplift and inspire. The scriptures offer many references to music being used as a form of worship, to express love, praise and devotion. The book of Psalms is a book of hymns. In it we read: "O sing unto the LORD a new song; for he hath done marvellous things . . . Make a joyful noise unto the LORD, all the earth: make a loud noise, and rejoice, and sing praise" (Psalms 98:1, 4), "Serve the LORD with gladness: come before his presence with singing" (Psalms 100:2) and "Sing unto him, sing psalms unto him" (Psalms 105:2).

A few months after The Church of Jesus Christ of Latter-day Saints was organized, through a revelation given to the prophet Joseph Smith, the Lord instructed Emma Smith to "make a selection of sacred hymns, as it shall be given thee, which is pleasing unto me, to be had in my church. For my soul delighteth in the song of the heart; yea, the song of the righteous is a prayer unto me, and it shall be answered with a blessing upon their heads" (D&C 25:11, 12).

In the preface of our hymnbook, the First Presidency wrote: "Hymns can lift our spirits, give us courage and move us to righteous action. They can fill our souls with heavenly thoughts and bring us a spirit of peace. Hymns can also help us withstand the temptations of the adversary. We encourage you to memorize your favorite hymns and study the scriptures that relate to them. Then, if unworthy thoughts enter your mind, sing a hymn to yourself, crowding out the evil with the good. . . . Let us memorize and ponder them, recite and sing them, and partake of their spiritual nourishment. Know that the song of the righteous is a prayer unto our Father in Heaven, 'and it shall be answered with a blessing upon [your] heads.'"[2]

Have you selected a theme song yet?

---

2. First Presidency Preface, *Hymns of The Church of Jesus Christ of Latter-Day Saints,* (Salt Lake City: The Church of Jesus Christ of Latter-day Saints, 1985), x.

Chapter 22

Make a Plan

Your Personal Truth

- Are you living the life you planned?
- Is daydreaming about your mission in life enough to motivate you to achieve it?
- What is your ultimate goal?
- What have you done today to help you obtain your ultimate goal?

A goal is a standard or final purpose that a person aspires to reach or accomplish. A goal is stronger than a dream, which implies fantasy. A goal represents a skill, ideal, or destination we are aiming toward, and which with conviction and determination, we will achieve. Civil rights hero Rosa Parks wrote: "I have learned over the years that when one's mind is made up, this diminishes the fear; knowing what must be done does away with fear."

Like an arrow aimed at a target, when we visualize a goal we move toward it. Napoleon Hill realized the power of visualization and said, "Whatever your mind can conceive and believe, it can achieve."

Some goals, like exercising daily or reading a book, may be accomplished in a short time. Other goals, such as graduating from college or saving money to buy a new car, may take years. Eternal goals are lifetime pursuits and may require additional effort after mortality.

In setting our goals, we should begin with our ultimate goal and set intermediate goals to help us advance toward that purpose. It has been said, "if we don't know where we are going, it doesn't matter which road we take."

Latter-day Saints are blessed to know what we ultimately want to achieve. The Savior has told us: "Seek ye first the kingdom of God . . . and all these things shall be added unto you" (Matthew 6:33 and 3 Nephi 13:33). Our ultimate goal is exaltation—to be "heirs of God, and joint-heirs with Christ" (Romans 8:17) of "all that [our] Father hath" (D&C 84:38).

Our goals should help us lead happy and productive lives, striving to become worthy to return to our Heavenly Father's presence. President Spencer W. Kimball has advised, "To be sure your life will be full and abundant, you must plan your life."[1]

With our ultimate goal in mind, each smaller goal should point in the same direction. English novelist and scholar J.R.R. Tolkien wrote: "Little by little, one travels far." No matter how small the task, each accomplished goal should move us closer to exaltation.

It is crucial that we do not waste our mortal existence by not having a plan. Elder Thomas S. Monson counseled: "No plan. No objective. No goal. The road to anywhere is the road to nowhere, and the road to nowhere leads to dreams sacrificed, opportunities squandered, and a life unfulfilled."[2]

Focus your mind on what you want to achieve. Set goals—today—that will help you become the person you want to be. "It is never too late to be what you might have been."[3]

An old Chinese proverb offers this advice: "The journey of a thousand miles begins with one step."

Do you have a plan that can lead you to eternal life?

---

1. Spencer W. Kimball, "Planning for a Full and Abundant Life," *Ensign,* May 1974, 86.
2. Thomas S. Monson, "Which Road Will You Travel?" *Ensign,* November 1976, 51.
3. George Eliot, writer.

Make a Plan

Dares to Improve Your Life

- With your ultimate goal in mind, I dare you to plan your life a week, a month, a year, 5 and 10 years into the future.
- I dare you to study your patriarchal blessing and pray for assistance in setting your goals.
- I dare you to write down clearly defined goals and set smaller goals to accomplish them.
- I dare you to select a goal to work on and do something each day for a month toward achieving it.

Setting goals should be a prayerful act. Who better knows our potential than the One who has created us? Heavenly Father has told us His goal is "to bring to pass the immortality and eternal life of man" (Moses 1:39). He wants us to be successful, and He will help us if we ask Him. President Gordon B. Hinckley has counseled: "Prayer unlocks the powers of heaven in our behalf . . . You cannot reach your potential alone. You need the help of the Lord."[1]

A great tool our Father in Heaven has provided to help us set goals is our patriarchal blessing. "A patriarchal blessing is the inspired and prophetic statement of your life's mission together with blessings, cautions, and admonitions as the patriarch may be prompted to give,"[2] explained President Ezra Taft Benson. As we prayerfully study and ponder our patriarchal blessing, the Lord will reveal to us "line upon line, precept upon precept" (D&C 98:12) our mission in life and the path we must to travel to realize it.

---

1. Gordon B. Hinckley, *Pittsburgh Pennsylvania Regional Conference,* April 28, 1996.
2. Ezra Taft Benson, "To the 'Youth of the Noble Birthright,'" *Ensign,* May 1986, 43-44.

With our goals firmly set, we must strive daily to achieve them, with an understanding that any progress, no matter how small, is moving us closer to our aspirations. Elder Joseph B. Wirthlin likened goals to running a marathon: "In some respects, progressing through life is like running a marathon. . . . [It] requires a good start and a strong, consistent effort all of the way to the finish. Just as marathon runners set explicit goals, so should each of us, look ahead and decide what we want to do with our lives . . . fix clearly in our minds what we want to be or what we want to be doing one year from now, five years, ten years, and beyond . . . Our ultimate goal should be eternal life—the kind of life God lives, the greatest of all the gifts of God. After we visualize ourselves as we would like to be in five, ten, or twenty years from now, we should identify the preparation we will need and determine to pay the price in effort, money, study, and prayer."[3]

Once our goals are set, we should periodically evaluate our progress and redefine our objectives. "To live righteous lives and accomplish the purpose of our creation, we must constantly review the past, determine our present status, and set goals for the future. Without this process there is little chance of reaching one's objectives,"[4] advised Elder O. Leslie Stone.

With clear objectives, set and worked toward with the Lord's help, we will see success. President Gordon B. Hinckley has said: "Never forget that you came to earth as a child of the divine Father, with something of divinity in your very makeup. The Lord did not send you here to fail. He did not give you life to waste it. He bestowed upon you the gift of mortality that you might gain experience—positive, wonderful, purposeful experience—that will lead to life eternal."[5]

Are you becoming the person you want to be?

---

3. Joseph B. Wirthlin, *Finding Peace in Our Lives,* (Salt Lake City: Deseret Book Co., 1995), 148.
4. O. Leslie Stone, "Making Your Marriage Successful," *Ensign,* May 1978, 57.
5. Gordon B. Hinckley, "How Can I Become the Woman of Whom I Dream?" *Ensign,* May 2001, 93; and *New Era,* November 2001, 4.

Chapter 23

How Great Thou Art

Your Personal Truth

- Do you revel in the beauty of God's handiwork?
- When did you last stop what you were doing and take the time to really enjoy watching a sunset?
- What thing of beauty did you thank God for today?
- Have you ever shared your feelings of gratitude for God's creations with another person?

A kind and loving Heavenly Father created a beautiful world for His children to live and learn in. All around are grand and glorious expressions of His love: horses running in a field, wildflowers nodding at the side of the road, the lilting song of a bird, blue skies hung with fluffy white clouds; the intense orange, pink and lavender hues of a sunset.

What pleasure it must give Him to see us revel in the beauty of His creations and appreciate His genius. To sing with the Psalmist and "Give unto the Lord the glory due unto his name; worship the Lord in the beauty of holiness" (Psalms 29:2).

"Was it not the Creator of the worlds who called our attention to the beauty of the lilies, the power in the tiny mustard seed, and the leaves on the fig tree?" asks Elder Neal A. Maxwell. "Was it not that same Creator who also asked us, as we observe the heavens, planets, and stars moving in their orbits, to remember that when we have so observed, we have 'seen God moving in his majesty and power' (D&C 88:47)? . . . Indeed, appreciation for the world (and all in it) which God has given us is but a prelude to adoration of the God who has so gloriously displayed His creativity for us."[1]

---

1. Neal A. Maxwell, "Creativity," *New Era*, August 1982, 4.

The words of the hymn "How Great Thou Art!" beautifully express the wonder and gratitude we should carry in our hearts:

When thru the woods and forest glades I wander,
And hear the birds sing sweetly in the trees,
When I look down from lofty mountain grandeur
And hear the brook and feel the gentle breeze,
Then sings my soul, my Savior God, to thee,
How great thou art! How great thou art!

O Lord my God, when I in awesome wonder
Consider all the worlds thy hands have made,
I see the stars, I hear the rolling thunder,
Thy pow'r throughout the universe displayed;
Then sings my soul, my Savior God, to thee,
How great thou art! How great thou art![2]

Do God's creations make your soul want to sing, "How great thou art"?

---

2. *Hymns of The Church of Jesus Christ of Latter-Day Saints,* (Salt Lake City: The Church of Jesus Christ of Latter-day Saints, 1985), no. 86.

How Great Thou Art

Dares to Improve Your Life

- I dare you to take time this evening to experience watching a sunset with the thought in mind that you must then describe it to someone who has never seen a sunset before. Afterward, call a friend and describe what you saw and felt while watching the sunset.

- Each day, for one week, I dare you to stop and enjoy God's handiwork. Find a cloud in the shape of a monster, discover a new star in the night's sky, smell roses along your way.

- I dare you to share your latest discovery of God's handiwork with another person—bear testimony of His creation.

- In each prayer, I dare you to thank Heavenly Father for beautiful creations—with a sincere heart, tell Him how much you enjoy His gifts.

A young child knelt in prayer and thanked God for His many blessings including, "clouds that look like monsters, a rainbow in the sky at the end of a rainy day, a robin's nest, the smell of fresh mowed grass, and a dog named Spot." This humble child recognized that "Heavens and earth are the Lord's handiwork" (D&C 104:14) and reveled in all of His creations.

Suppose you gave a beautiful gift—red roses, a moving piece of music, a new baseball glove, a favorite dessert, a warm sweater, aftershave or perfume—and the recipient thoughtlessly accepted it with little or no recognition. How would it make you feel to have your gift go unappreciated?

When we do not stop to take pleasure in all God's glorious handiwork and thank Him for the beauty all around us, it is as if we have unappreciatively set aside His gifts.

A Psalm of David asks, "When I consider thy heavens, the work of thy fingers, the moon and the stars, which thou hast ordained; What is man, that thou art mindful of him?" (Psalms 8:3-4). The Lord answers, "For mine own purpose have I made these things. . . . For behold, this is my work and my glory—to bring to pass the immortality and eternal life of man" (Moses 1:32, 39). We are His ultimate creation and it is for our pleasure He created the earth and all things upon it.

"When we look to see the evidence of creation all around us, from a grain of sand to the majestic planets, we begin to realize that we are the greatest of all God's creations," explains Elder M. Russell Ballard. ". . . God created the earth in all its magnificent glory, not as an end in itself, but for us, his children. . . . We sometimes feel great respect and reverence for creative genius as expressed in great art or music. How much more should we revere the power and majesty of our Divine Creator?"[1]

Will you praise and honor your Heavenly Father by taking time to enjoy His magnificent creations, and bear testimony of His handiwork today?

---

1. M. Russell Ballard, "God's Love for His Children," *Ensign*, May 1988, 57.

Chapter 24

One Can Make a Difference

Your Personal Truth

- Can one person truly make a difference in the world?
- Is the world a better place because you are in it?
- Do Latter-day Saints have a responsibility to make a difference in the lives of others?
- What is one thing that you can do today to make the world a better place to live in?

"I am only one, but still I am one," wrote Edward Everett Hale. Each of us possesses unique talents and skills that can contribute to making the world a better place and bless the lives of those we come in contact with. The question is not whether we can do something that makes a difference, but will we?

In the film *It's a Wonderful Life,* the principal character of the movie, George Bailey, feels alone and discouraged by the presumably hopeless state of his life. In his darkest hour, Clarence, his guardian angel, intervenes to show Bailey that his seemingly unimportant gestures have made a profound difference in the lives of many, many people.

Compassion and love for our fellowman are fundamental in making a difference in the world. Jude, the brother of James, admonished: "Have compassion, making a difference" (Jude 1:22). As we share our time, talents and resources we learn to be more compassionate and Christlike.

Heavenly Father needs us to make a difference in people's lives. It is through others that He often meets our needs—and through us that others' prayers are answered. He has given us limitless opportunities to make a difference: temple service, sharing the gospel, magnifying our callings, family history, visiting and home teaching,

103

humanitarian aid projects, paying a generous fast offering, delivering a meal to someone in need, listening, being a friend, and so much more.

Within our neighborhoods and communities are many people in need of assistance. Some of the organizations or projects that almost always need volunteers include: literacy programs, hospices, disaster relief agencies, homes for elderly or mentally challenged, museums and libraries, schools, companionship programs for underprivileged children and the elderly.

Making a difference can be as simple as a kind word, a friendly smile or setting a good example. Before a football game, one young man suggested offering a prayer. His teammates and coaches agreed and made it a regular part of their pre-game meeting. A PTA mom started an "Esteem Team" at her daughter's middle school. Once each month, the teens meet after school to perform acts of kindness for the student body and the community.

Plant a tree in your neighborhood, give another driver your parking space, write a letter of encouragement, work in a soup kitchen, tutor a teenager or teach someone to read, bake someone a birthday cake when it's not their day, pick-up trash, learn the names of all you come in contact with.

Hales further writes: "I cannot do everything, but still I can do something; and because I cannot do everything, I will not refuse to do the something that I can do."

What is the one something you will do today?

One Can Make a Difference

"As the old man walked the beach at dawn he noticed a youth ahead of him picking up starfish and flinging them into the sea. Finally, catching up with the youth, he asked him why he was doing this. The answer was that the stranded starfish would die if left in the morning sun. 'But the beach goes on for miles and there are millions of starfish,' countered the old man. 'How can your effort make any difference?' The young man looked at the starfish in his hand and then threw it to the safety of the waves. 'It makes a difference to this one,' he said."[1]

The gospel of Jesus Christ is one of individual responsibility. What we do matters. Our actions have eternal consequences. Charity and compassion are essential to our salvation. The Lord commanded, "except ye have charity ye can in nowise be saved in the kingdom of God;" (Moroni 10:21).

We can make a difference, not only in our own lives, but also in the lives of those around us. We can and we must. President Gordon

---

1. Brian Cavanaugh, *The Sower's Seeds.*

B. Hinckley said: "No man or woman proceeds alone. All of us are largely the products of the lives which touch upon our lives."[2]

Throughout the world, Latter-day Saints are making a difference in their homes, their neighborhoods, their communities, and in their nations. They are serving food in shelters for the homeless, making humanitarian aid packages, sewing clothing and making quilts for those in need, raising money for charities, helping in disaster relief efforts.

They are changing laws, laboring against abortion, pornography and gambling, helping elect good men and women to public office, or running for office themselves. They are members of the PTA, serving as teacher's aids, shaping school curricula. They are babysitting while couples attend the temple, raking leaves and shoveling snow in the yards of the elderly, writing letters to missionaries. They are setting an example of righteousness and sharing the gospel of salvation with others. Most are ordinary people, making a difference one person at a time.

It does not matter how young or old you are, you can do something that will make a difference in the world. President Hinckley said: "The major work of the world is not done by geniuses. It is done by ordinary people who have learned to work in an extraordinary manner."[3]

They have learned the simple truth, that "The purpose of life is a life of purpose."

William Penn wrote: "If there is any kindness I can show, or any good thing I can do to any fellow being, let me do it now, and not deter or neglect it, as I shall not pass this way again."

The question is not *if* you can do something, but *will* you?

---

2. Gordon B. Hinckley, *Stand A Little Taller,* (Salt Lake City: Eagle Gate, 2001), 295.
3. Gordon B. Hinckley, "Our Fading Civility," BYU commencement address, 25 Apr. 1996, 15.

Chapter 25

The Miracle of Faith

Your Personal Truth

- How do you rate the strength of your faith?
- How does your faith in Heavenly Father and Jesus Christ give you hope?
- What evidence is there that God is aware of your life and daily circumstances?
- Do you seek to solve your own problems, or do you have the faith to invite God to help you?

On dark and stormy days, when you can't see the sun, it is still there shining above the turbulence. If you have ever flown in an airplane when the sky was overcast, you learn this simple truth. On the ground all you see are dark clouds, but as the plane climbs above them, you discover the sun is shining brightly. When we find ourselves in the midst of stormy trials and all seems bleak and gloomy, we must remember that once we climb above the clouds we will see that the sun is still shining.

Our faith in God's Son, Jesus Christ, is the vehicle that enables us to rise above the negative elements in our life. The Savior is our comfort, our protection, and our light that shines above the storms of life. His gospel provides safety and security.

The prophet Joseph Smith experienced many storms in his life. During one of his darkest moments he prayed, "O God, where art thou? And where is the pavilion that covereth thy hiding place?" (D&C 121:1). Joseph knew his plea was heard. He knew the Lord had understanding of his pain, born of His own experience. As he lifted his voice, the comforting promise came: "My son, peace be unto thy soul; thine adversity and thine afflictions shall be but a small moment;

And then, if thou endure it well, God shall exalt thee on high; thou shalt triumph over all thy foes" (D&C 121:7-8).

In his own hour of darkness, the Lord offered words of comfort to His faithful followers: "Peace I leave with you, my peace I give unto you: not as the world giveth, give I unto you. Let not your heart be troubled, neither let it be afraid" (John 14:27). "These great words of confidence are a beacon to each of us," said President Gordon B. Hinckley. "In him we may indeed have trust. For he and his promises will never fail."[1]

In the midst of life's storms, some doubt because they cannot reason how God will answer their petition. They do not understand that He may be working on their behalf in ways they do not yet recognize. A perfect knowledge of how God will accomplish miracles in our lives does not require any faith. Faith is knowing the sun is still shining above the clouds, even though you cannot see it. "God will open the way," President Hinckley assures. "When there is no way, He will open the way. I am satisfied of that."[2]

Faith in our Heavenly Father and Jesus Christ will comfort and direct us safely through all of life's storms, to rise above them and know that "after much tribulation come the blessings" (D&C 58:4).

In the midst of personal storms and darkness, do you have faith in God and His Son?

---

1. Gordon B. Hinckley, "The Continuing Pursuit of Truth," *Ensign,* April 1986, 2.
2. "Excerpts from Recent Addresses of President Gordon B. Hinckley," *Ensign,* December 1995, 66.

The Miracle of Faith

Dares to Improve Your Life

- Each day for a week, or longer, I dare you to read a story of faith from the scriptures.

- I dare you to strengthen your faith by praying and fasting with a specific purpose in mind, believing God will answer your plea.

- For a week, I dare you to read daily about Christ's ministry and note scriptures about faith.

- I dare you to keep a miracle journal: record each answer to prayer and evidence of the Lord's hand in your life.

In the depths of despair, discouragement, loneliness, loss, heartbreak, unfairness and other adversity, our faith in Heavenly Father and Jesus Christ is tested. Faith demands that we conquer our fear, relinquish our inability to reason and control circumstances, and submit ourselves to the will of God. President Harold B. Lee wisely instructed, "You must learn to walk to the edge of the light, and then a few steps into the darkness, then the light will appear and show the way before you."[1]

Faith has been called a principle of power. It is the basic source for accessing God's strength in our behalf. The scriptures illustrate faith in action: Noah built an ark and saved his family from the flood (see Hebrews 11:7); Sara conceived Isaac in her old age (see Hebrews 11:11); Moses parted the Red Sea (see Hebrews 11:29); "by faith the walls of Jericho fell down" (Hebrews 11:30); Nephi obtained the Brass Plates (see 1 Nephi 3-4); and because of his faith, the brother of Jared saw the finger of the Lord touch the stones that would light the way to the land of promise (see Ether 3:4-6). These stories and those

---

1. Quoted by Boyd K. Packer, "The Edge of the Light," address delivered at Brigham Young University, Provo, Utah, 4 March 1990.

of other scriptural heros and heroines teach us that nothing is impossible if we have faith in the Lord.

Jesus taught, "If ye have faith as a grain of mustard seed, ye shall say unto this mountain, Remove hence to yonder place; and it shall remove; and nothing shall be impossible unto you" (Matthew 17:20).

The Lord wants to help us, and He has promised to do so if we are faithful and obedient. President George Q. Cannon explained: "When we went forth into the waters of baptism and covenanted with our Father in heaven to serve Him and keep His commandments, He bound Himself also by covenant to us that He would never desert us, never leave us to ourselves, never forget us, that in the midst of trials and hardships, when everything was arrayed against us, He would be near unto us and would sustain us. That was His covenant."[2] If we put our faith and trust in Him, and strive to obey His commandments, we need not fear.

When the Lord asked the brother of Jared "Believest thou the words which I shall speak" (Ether 3:11), He was not asking him to believe what He had already told him, but to commit himself to something that had not yet happened. Faith is not faith if we know the outcome. Elder Boyd K. Packer said: "Faith, to be faith, must center around something that is not known. Faith, to be faith, must go beyond that for which there is confirming evidence. Faith, to be faith, must go into the unknown. Faith, to be faith, must walk to the edge of the light, and then a few steps into the darkness. If everything has to be known, if everything has to be explained, if everything has to be certified, then there is no need for faith. Indeed, there is no room for it."[3]

Do you have room for faith in your life?

---

2. George Q. Cannon, *Gospel Truth: Discourses and Writings of President George Q. Cannon,* selected, arranged, and edited by Jerreld L. Newquist (Salt Lake City: Deseret Book Co., 1987), 134.

3. Boyd K. Packer, "Faith," *Improvement Era,* November 1968, 62.

Chapter 26

Choose Good Habits

Your Personal Truth

- Are good and bad habits inherited?
- What is your worst bad habit, and how does it make you feel about yourself?
- What good habits would you most like to possess?
- Do thoughts have the power to affect your habits?

We do not inherit fixed habits and a noble character, nor do our circumstances impose them upon us. Instead, we come into mortality with the privileged gift of choice. The choices we make over and over, again and again, become habits that form our character. We can become slaves to bad habits, or we can choose to develop good ones. Benjamin Franklin astutely shared, "It is easier to prevent bad habits than to break them."

Expanding on this idea, President Joseph Fielding Smith taught, ". . . it is not easy to tell the truth, if you have been a confirmed liar. It is not easy to be honest, if you have formed habits of dishonesty."[1]

The repetitious practice of good habits fortifies us against the temptation to break commandments. For example, a person who always keeps the Sabbath Day holy will find it easier to resist temptation to participate in sports or other recreational activities on Sunday. The habit of never gossiping strengthens our resolve to never speak unkindly of others.

Elder Delbert L. Stapley counseled, "We should become so involved in acquiring good quality traits and participating in character-building activities that there is no time to engage in anything

---

1. Joseph Fielding Smith, *The Way to Perfection* (Salt Lake City: Genealogical Society of Utah, 1949), 149.

111

worthless or harmful. Our habits should be those that make us susceptible to faith and testimony. One of the best habits to be cultivated is that of reading the scriptures to become knowledgeable of our responsibilities. By learning God's commandments and keeping them, we develop the ways of righteousness that are an expression of our faith. With good habits we prepare ourselves for excellence. We need to ask ourselves, 'Are my usual thoughts and present actions worthy of eternal life?'"[2]

The toughest battles fought are within our own mind, as we learn to choose good over evil. C. A. Hall wrote: "We sow our thoughts, and we reap our actions; we sow our actions, and we reap our habits; we sow our habits, and we reap our characters; we sow our characters, and we reap our destiny."[3] Each victory, no matter how small or large the conquest, determines our ultimate happiness: "He that overcometh shall inherit all things" (Revelation 21:7).

All habits, both good and evil, start with a single decision—we decide to give in to temptation or to overcome it. Each choice made over and over, again and again becomes a defeat or a victory. Wise king Solomon said, "He that ruleth his spirit [is mightier] than he that taketh a city" (Proverbs 16:32).

Are you in the habit of choosing a noble character?

---

2. Delbert L. Stapley, "Good Habits Develop Good Character," *Ensign*, November 1974, 20.
3. C. A. Hall, *The Home Book of Quotations*, (New York: Dodd, Mead & Company, 1935), 845.

Choose Good Habits

Dares to Improve Your Life

- I dare you to quit your worst bad habit for an hour—then a day. As your resolve increases, quit for a longer period of time until you have eliminated it from your character.

- I dare you to build on small victories until they become conquests, and your worst bad habit no longer exists.

- I dare you to call on God for help with each battle and thank Him for the victory.

- I dare you to replace a bad habit with a good one—each time you feel the urge to return to your former habit, perform your new one in its place.

The repetitious acts of our daily lives form habits, good or bad. If we are not watchful, too quickly a bad choice becomes routine, and soon we are servants to our evil habits. Horace Mann wrote, "Habit is a cable; we weave a thread of it a day, and at last we cannot break it."

Evil habits destroy our character and can ruin our life. Each time we surrender to sin our resistance is broken down and it becomes easier to repeat the offense and yield to other temptations. Over time it becomes more and more difficult to resist evil actions, until eventually the desire to sin is so strong it is almost impossible to resist. Addiction to a long-practiced vice is so strong that people can long to free themselves of its chain, yet yearn to repeat the habit. Lehi understood the restrictive shackles of evil habits and pled with his sons, "Shake off the chains with which ye are bound, and come forth out of obscurity, and arise from the dust" (2 Nephi 1:23).

"Who among us hasn't felt the chains of bad habits?" asked Elder Marvin J. Ashton. "These habits may have impeded our progress, may have made us forget who we are, may have destroyed our self-image, may have put our family life in jeopardy, and may have hindered our ability to serve our fellowmen and our God. So many of us tend to say, "This is the way I am. I can't change. I can't throw off the chains of habit."[1]

Our Heavenly Father wants us to develop self-mastery so that we can overcome our weaknesses. As recorded in the Book of Mormon, He has given us this promise: "And if men come unto me I will show unto them their weakness. I give unto men weakness that they may be humble; and my grace is sufficient for all men that humble themselves before me; for if they humble themselves before me, and have faith in me, then will I make weak things become strong unto them" (Ether 12:27).

Like all skills, self-mastery is developed through practice. The repeated action of resisting temptation strengthens our resolve.

It is easier to break a bad habit if we replace it with a good one. "We have a gracious, kind, and loving Father in Heaven who stands ready to help us," wrote Delbert L. Stapley. "Self-mastery, self-control, and self-discipline are required strengths that enable us to set aside temptations to do wrong. It is a wonderful feeling to conquer wrong practices and to be free and unencumbered from their detrimental effects, both physically and spiritually. When we have conquered our bad habits and replaced them with good ones, living as we should, obedient and faithful, then we are on our way to the presence of God."[2]

Nathaniel Emmons wisely said: "Habit is the best of servants, or the worst of masters."

Are you the slave or master of your habits?

---

1. Marvin J. Ashton, "Shake Off the Chains with Which Ye Are Bound," *Ensign*, November 1986, 13.
2. Delbert L. Stapley, "Good Habits Develop Good Character," *Ensign*, November 1974, 20.

Chapter 27

Friendship

Your Personal Truth

- Do other people consider you to be a good friend?
- Do you know the details of your friend's lives? Their birth date, anniversary date, names of children or siblings, favorite color and food, important events in their lives?
- Do you always speak highly of your friends when you speak of them to others?
- Do you live your life in such a way that causes your friends to thank Heavenly Father for a friend like you?

For centuries, musicians, philosophers, poets, writers and friends have spoken of that blessed connection between hearts called friendship. Ideally, our family ought to be among our closest friends. True friends sustain us.

An unknown author profoundly wrote, "A friend hears the song in my heart and sings it to me when my memory fails." Friends help us seek and find the truth, motivate us, listen, bear our burden with us, help keep us moving in the right direction, offer a safe harbor, and love us unconditionally.

Of building friendships, Elder Marvin J. Ashton taught, "A friend is a possession we earn, not a gift."[1] The Lord said, "Ye are my friends, if ye do whatsoever I command you. Henceforth I call you not my servants; for the servant knoweth not what his lord doeth: but I have called you friend; for all things that I have heard of my Father I have made known unto you" (John 15:13-15). *Studies in Scriptures* further explains, "The close relationship of the Lord to his faithful servants is shown in his greeting them as friends. A servant carries out orders as he is commanded. A 'friend' is one with whom the Lord confides his purposes and plans."[2]

---

1. Marvin J. Ashton, "What Is a Friend?" *Ensign*, January 1973, 41.

Several references to the Lord's friends are found in the scriptures. "The friend of the bridegroom" is the one that "standeth and heareth him, [and] rejoiceth greatly because of the bridegroom's voice" (John 3:29). For his righteousness, Abraham "was called the Friend of God" (James 2:33). In latter-day revelation we learn that the Lord said to the prophet Joseph Smith and his associates, "And again I say unto you, my friends, for from henceforth I shall call you friends, it is expedient that I give unto you this commandment, that ye become even as my friends in days when I was with them, traveling to preach the gospel in my power;" (D&C 84:77) and "I will call you my friends, for you are my friends, and ye shall have an inheritance with me" (D&C 93:34).

A further examination of these and other scriptures teaches that the friends of the Savior are those who are obedient, faithful, loyal, trustworthy, kind, charitable—those who have earned the right to be called friends. Is it any different with our own friends? Do we not earn the right to have a friend by being faithful, loyal, trustworthy, kind and charitable?

We can learn how to be a friend from the scriptures. A man preparing to move his family to a new town asked one of the residents, "What kind of people live in this community?" The wise resident asked, "What kind of people lived in the town you are moving from?" The man brightly answered, "They were wonderful people, kind and friendly. They were good neighbors, good citizens, and good Christians." The wise resident answered, "That is the kind of people you will find in this town—and every city you live in." Another man, also moving his family to the town asked the same resident, "What kind of people live in this town?" The wise resident asked, "What kind of people lived in the town you are moving from?" The man answered, "They were disagreeable people. That is the reason we are moving. They were gossips, poor neighbors, unkind and unfriendly." The wise resident answered, "You will find that same kind of people in our town, and in every town you live in."

Wise King Solomon wrote: "A man that hath friends must shew himself friendly" (Proverbs 18:24).

Are you worthy of having good friends?

---

2. Ed. Robert L. Millet and Kent P. Jackson, *Studies in Scriptures, Vol. 1: The Doctrine and Covenants,* (Salt Lake City: Deseret Book Co., 1989), 342.

Friendship

Dares to Improve Your Life

- I dare you to sincerely pray to become a better friend.

- I dare you to call a friend and listen—each time you are tempted to talk about yourself, ask your friend another question and really listen to the answer.

- This week, I dare you to discover that any task is easier with the help of a friend by assisting your friend with a household chore, washing or fixing their car, weeding a garden, completing a homework assignment, cooking a meal, painting a room, or cleaning out the garage.

- This month, I dare you to discover a burden your friend is carrying and do something tangible (not just saying, "If you need anything, call") to help them shoulder the weight.

Ralph Waldo Emerson wrote: "The glory of friendship is not the outstretched hand, nor the kindly smile, nor the joy of companionship; it is the spiritual inspiration that comes to one when he discovers that someone else believes in him and is willing to trust him with his friendship."

We all need friends—good friends, who take the time to know us, to be with us, to listen to us, to uplift and inspire us, to help shoulder our burdens, to love us. Lucy Mack Smith is attributed with saying, "Watch over one another . . . that we may all sit down in heaven together."[1]

While the prophet Joseph Smith was incarcerated in Liberty Jail, the Lord gave him these comforting words, "Thy friends do stand by thee, and they shall hail thee again with warm hearts and friendly hands" (D&C 121:9). Knowing that his friends stood by him gave the prophet comfort and strength.

---

1. *Minutes of the Female Relief Society of Nauvoo, 24 March 1842,* Archives of The Church of Jesus Christ of Latter-day Saints, Salt Lake City, Utah.

Joseph had earned the right to have good friends, because he was a good friend. Toward the end of his life he said, "If my life is of no value to my friends, it is of no value to myself."[2]

By building up our friends we build ourselves into better people. President Lorenzo Snow taught: "Now an individual, in order to secure the highest and greatest blessings to himself, . . . let him go to work and be willing to sacrifice for the benefit of his friends."[3]

The Savior said, "Greater love hath no man than this, that a man lay down his life for his friends" (John 15:13). Indeed, He loved His friends so deeply He did lay down His life. None of us can compare to such love and sacrifice, but we can draw this lesson from the Savior's example: we show our love for our friends by giving daily of our time, attention and resources.

Speaking of the sanctity of friendship, President David O. McKay said, "Next to a sense of kinship with God come the helpfulness, encouragement, and inspiration of friends. Friendship is a sacred possession. As air, water, and sunshine to flowers, trees, and verdure, so smiles, sympathy, and love of friends to the daily life of man! 'To live, laugh, love one's friends, and be loved by them is to bask in the sunshine of life.'"[4]

Singer and songwriter Carole King composed these beautiful words about friendship:

> *You just call out my name / And you know wherever I am*
> *I'll come runnin' to see you again / Winter, spring, summer or fall*
> *All you have to do is call / And I'll be there. / You've got a friend.*[5]

Do you have a friend who would come runnin' if you called?

Would *you* come runnin' if your friend called?

---

2. *History of the Church, Period I,* vol. vi, 549.
3. Lorenzo Snow, *The Teachings of Lorenzo Snow,* edited by Clyde J. Williams (Salt Lake City: Bookcraft, 1984), 148.
4. David O. McKay, *Gospel Ideals: Selections from the Discourses of David O. McKay* (Salt Lake City: *Improvement Era,* 1953), 253.
5. Carole King, "You've Got A Friend."

Chapter 28

Joyful Living

Your Personal Truth

- What joys have you experienced today?
- Do you believe you are worthy of experiencing joy each day of your life?
- Do you have control over the amount of joy you experience in life, or do you depend more upon your family, friends and circumstances to make you feel happy?
- When was the last time you felt real joy—the tingle of pure delight?

This very moment is your life. Our daily experiences—good and bad, happy and sad—are life itself. Often we spend too much time worrying or dreaming about tomorrow, next week, next year, or the distant future, instead of focusing on the joy of the moment.

Boris Pasternak wrote: "Man is born to live and not to prepare to live." This is it. There is no dress rehearsal for life. The curtain has already gone up—it's time to revel in your own performance.

Feeling joy in our daily lives can be learned and practiced like any other skill. It begins by becoming aware of our actions and reactions. As you go about your daily tasks, notice Fall leaves turning from green to mustard, orange, rust and brown; listen to music you love, and sing along with familiar tunes; smell the salt water carried in the breeze from the ocean; savor ice cold lemonade on a humid summer day. Write with your favorite pen on paper you have saved for something special, buy or pick fresh flowers to have in your office or home, take photographs of family and friends to frame and display. Kiss your spouse, hug your mom and dad, hold a baby in your arms, turn off your cell phone and be still. Be present. Experience the moment. *Carpe Diem*—seize the day!

The Lord has said: "Wherefore, lift up thy heart and rejoice . . ." (D&C 25:13). As members of Christ's church we have so much to be joyful about. President Gordon B. Hinckley has said: "The gospel is a thing of joy. It provides us with a reason for gladness. Of course there are times of sorrow. Of course there are hours of concern and anxiety. We all worry, but the Lord has told us to lift our hearts and rejoice. I see so many people . . . who seem never to see the sunshine, but who constantly walk with storms under cloudy skies. Cultivate an attitude of happiness. Cultivate a spirit of optimism. Walk with faith, rejoicing in the beauties of nature, in the goodness of those you love, in the testimony which you carry in your heart concerning things divine."[1]

We must stop viewing life as a long, hard, uphill climb and start enjoying the adventure of the journey: revel in a sunset with someone, listen to a family member, laugh with a friend, sing a duet, dance in the kitchen, read to a child, play a game of catch, telephone your mother, share your testimony, live joyfully!

What one thing will you find today to "lift up [your] heart and rejoice" about?

---

1. Gordon B. Hinckley, "If Thou Art Faithful," *Ensign,* November 1984, 89.

Joyful Living

Dares to Improve Your Life

- I dare you to write down 50 things that bring you joy.
- For a week, I dare you to make a daily list of the things that bring you joy.
- At the end of the week, I dare you to hang the list—near a mirror, beside your computer, on the refrigerator—to remind yourself of all that is joyous in your life.
- I dare you to thank God each morning and every night for the joys of your life.

Joy is bigger than contentment, more intense than gladness—it is a feeling so vast that it almost overwhelms you. Ultimate joy is a sensation of well-being that comes from exercising faith in the Lord Jesus Christ and obeying God's commandments.

Elder Richard G. Scott said: "Your joy in life depends upon your trust in Heavenly Father and His holy Son, your conviction that their plan of happiness truly can bring you joy."[1]

We were all present at the great council in heaven when the wondrous plan of salvation was unveiled. The scriptures say, "the morning stars sang together," and we "shouted for joy" (Job 38:7). We would be given the opportunity to come into mortality and strive to achieve a "fulness of joy." Think of the celebration that must have ensued: imagine your merriest Christmas, happiest birthday, most delightful New Year's Day and festive Fourth of July combined, then multiply that by a zillion times and the level of joy was still more wondrous.

Heavenly Father desires us to achieve the ultimate joy that will come through exaltation. As we are striving to achieve that goal, He

---

1. Richard G. Scott, "Finding Joy in Life," *Ensign*, May 1996, 24.

wants us to be happy and to experience joy in our daily mortal lives. He has told us, "Men are, that they might have joy" (2 Nephi 2:25). Notice that God did not say they *must* have joy or that they *will* have joy, but that they *might* have joy.

Our Father in Heaven wants us to have joy—but it is our choice to want it enough to do what is required to obtain it.

Jesus Christ exemplified the pattern for joyful living: He trusted Heavenly Father, obeyed His commandments, served others, and prayed for strength and direction. He instructed, "For I have given you an example, that ye should do as I have done to you . . . If ye know these things, happy are ye if ye do them" (John 13:15, 17).

President Gordon B. Hinckley has said: "Joy comes of service. Joy comes of growth and activity in the ways of the Lord. I urge upon you the great importance of moving forward, having ever before you the example of the Savior of all mankind, even Jesus Christ. Pray in His name every night. Pray in His name every morning; and during the day exemplify in all of your activities the great virtues which He taught. I do not hesitate to promise you that if you do this, you will be happy and your lives will be productive."[2]

The Savior told us what to do and showed us how to do it. The choice to live joyfully is ours.

How long has it been since you "shouted for joy?"

---

2. Gordon B. Hinckley, *Stand A Little Taller,* (Salt Lake City: Eagle Gate, 2001), 296.

Chapter 29

The Gift of Talents

Your Personal Truth

- Do you honestly believe that Heavenly Father has given you special gifts and talents?
- What talents would you like to develop this year? In five years? In ten?
- Do you have a responsibility to discover your talents and use them to build God's kingdom?
- Can accepting responsibilities and assignments in the Church help increase your talents?

Our Father in Heaven has given each of us talents and gifts that will enrich our lives and help us fulfill our mission on earth, to build His kingdom and bless the lives of others.

Some tragically claim they have few or no talents because they cannot sing, dance, play music, paint, act, or play sports. They do not look beyond artistic areas and sports to discover that their special abilities may lie in teaching others, public speaking, being a friend, repairing automobiles, caring for young children, cooking delicious meals, leadership, organization, mathematics, enthusiasm, humor, science, sharing the gospel, decision-making, originality, communication, listening, compassion, and so forth.

Each of us is a unique individual with our own special set of gifts and talents. The Lord told the prophet Joseph Smith: "For all have not every gift given unto them; for there are many gifts, and to every man is given a gift by the Spirit of God. To some is given one, and to some is given another, that all may be profited thereby" (D&C 46:11-12).

Discovering and improving our talents requires desire and effort. We must humbly ask Heavenly Father to help us recognize and expand our talents. We should study our patriarchal blessings to identify our individual strengths and abilities. When set apart for a calling, listen for special gifts that are conferred upon you. Try something new—take a class in auto maintenance, swimming, accounting, flower arranging, or writing—you may uncover a hidden talent. Strive to become better at what you are already good at. Our talents may seem few or limited at first, but with hard work they will grow.

The Lord has said: "For what doth it profit a man if a gift is bestowed upon him, and he receive not the gift? Behold, he rejoices not in that which is given unto him, neither rejoices in him who is the giver of the gift" (D&C 88:33).

Recognition and expansion of our talents is a physical manifestation of our gratitude to God for His gifts. "Let your light so shine before men, that they may see your good works, and glorify your Father which is in heaven," (Matthew 5:16).

It is vital that we discover and develop our individual talents and gifts because God will hold us accountable for our stewardship of them. The Apostle Paul stated: "Neglect not the gift that is in thee" (1 Timothy 4:14).

In our dispensation, President Joseph F. Smith taught: "Every son and every daughter of God has received some talent, and each will be held to strict account for the use or misuse to which it is put."[1]

What will you report to Heavenly Father about your talent stewardship?

---

1. "The Returned Missionary," *Juvenile Instructor,* November 1903, 689.

The Gift of Talents

Dares to Improve Your Life

- I dare you to pray each day for Heavenly Father's help in recognizing and developing your talents.
- I dare you to study your patriarchal blessing and write down references to your gifts and instructions for their use.
- I dare you to write down the ten most important things you have accomplished in the last five years and the skills you used to achieve them.
- I dare you to select a talent you want to obtain, or develop further, and do something each day for a month to expand your skill.

Benjamin Franklin wisely counseled: "Hide not your talents, they for use were made. What's a sundial in the shade?"

Heavenly Father did not give us gifts and talents to be neglected or unappreciated. He not only wants us to use and expand them, He has commanded us to do so or they will be taken from us.

In the parable of the talents recorded in Matthew 25, the Lord teaches us to cultivate the gifts we are given or they will be taken from us: A man about to leave on a journey to a far country calls his servants together and commends to them his wealth. To one servant he gives five talents, to another he gives two, and to another, one talent, each according to his ability. While the master was away, the servants who received five and two talents doubled them, but the servant who received one dug a hole and hid it.

When the master returned, he called for the servants to give an accounting of the talents entrusted to each. To the servants who increased their talents he said, "Well done, thou good and faithful servant: thou hast been faithful over a few things, I will make thee ruler over many things: enter thou into the joy of thy lord" (verses 21 and 23).

The servant who was afraid to use his talent and hid it, he called "wicked and slothful," and he took "therefore the talent from him, and give it unto him which hath ten talents. For unto every one that hath shall be given, and he shall have abundance: but from him that hath not shall be taken away even that which he hath" (verses 28, 29).

Even the servant who received only one talent was expected to use it. It is the same with us. We must learn to recognize and delight in the use of the talents we have been blessed with. We cannot let fear or pride stop us from sharing them. William Blake wrote: "The woods would be very silent if no birds sang there except those that sang best."

Heavenly Father has blessed each of us with talents and skills: some have been given athletic ability, some can sing or play the piano, some are gifted teachers, while others are eloquent speakers, peacemakers, or strong leaders.

Elder L. Tom Perry of the Quorum of the Twelve Apostles, has said: "It matters not the size or the quantity but the effort we put forth to develop the talents and abilities we have received. You are not competing with anyone else. You are only competing with yourself to do the best with whatever you have received. Each talent that is developed will be greatly needed and will give you tremendous fulfillment and satisfaction during your life."[1]

Will the Lord call you "slothful" or will He say, "Well done, thou good and faithful servant?"

---

1. L. Tom Perry, "Youth of the Noble Birthright," *Ensign,* November 1998, 73.

Chapter 30

A Generous Fast Offering

Your Personal Truth

- Do you consider fast offerings an important part of living the law of the fast?
- Are you generous in paying your fast offering each month?
- Do you give with a joyous heart, realizing you are caring for the needs of your brothers and sisters?
- If the Lord were coming to your home for dinner, would your fast offering be enough to provide a meal for Him that you would be proud to serve?

We are given the opportunity to help those in need when we fast, pray and each month give an offering of food or the money we would have spent on the two meals we abstained from. When we consecrate our fast by giving a generous offering, we become partners with Heavenly Father in caring for the needs of others. Our offerings literally provide food, clothing, and shelter for our less fortunate brothers and sisters.

Consecrating a portion of the abundance Heavenly Father has given us to the assistance of others is an ancient principle. The Lord commanded Moses, "Thou shalt not harden thine heart, nor shut thine hand from thy poor brother: But thou shalt open thine hand wide unto him, and shalt surely lend him sufficient for his need" (Deuteronomy 15:7-8).

Generous payment of fast offerings demonstrates our love for the Lord, who said: "For inasmuch as ye do it unto the least of these, ye do it unto me" (D&C 42:38). Whereas, He warned that those who refuse to obey His command to care for the poor and needy are "not my disciple" (D&C 52:40).

What is an appropriate fast offering? Elder Russell M. Nelson instructed: "The generous offering to the bishop is understood to represent the financial equivalent of at least two meals. A liberal donation so reserved and dedicated to the poor is ennobling to the soul and helps one develop charity, one of the greatest attributes of a noble human character (see 1 Corinthians 13)."[1]

Eternal blessings come to those who remember the poor and needy. The Lord instructed his disciples to "give to the poor, and thou shalt have treasure in heaven" (Mark 10:21).

In our day, President Gordon B. Hinckley has said that if the principles of fast day and the fast offering were observed throughout the world, "the hungry would be fed, the naked clothed, the homeless sheltered. Our burden of taxes would be lightened. The giver would not suffer but would be blessed by [this] small abstinence. A new measure of concern and unselfishness would grow in the hearts of people everywhere. Can anyone doubt the divine wisdom that created this program which has blessed the people of this church as well as many who are not members of this church?"[2]

How much of a fast offering would you give if you knew that amount was going directly to help a member of your own family who was in need of assistance? Are we not all brothers and sisters in God's family?

---

1. Russell M. Nelson, "I Have a Question," *Ensign,* April 1976, 32.
2. Gordon B. Hinckley, "The State of the Church," *Ensign,* May 1991, 51.

A Generous Fast Offering

Dares to Improve Your Life

- I dare you to prayerfully consider the amount of your current fast offering contribution.
- I dare you to make the giving of fast offerings a fundamental part of your monthly fast.
- I dare you to prayerfully dedicate a fast to becoming aware of those in need, then make an appropriate fast offering.
- I dare you to become generous in your fast offerings—give more than the actual cost of the meals, give an amount that demonstrates your gratitude to God for His blessings.

Have you ever looked at the overwhelming need in the world and thought, "What can I do that could possibly make a difference?"

"I will tell you plainly one thing you can do," said Elder Joseph B. Wirthlin. "You can live the law of the fast and contribute a generous fast offering. Fast offerings are used for one purpose only: to bless the lives of those in need. Every dollar given to the bishop as a fast offering goes to assist the poor. When donations exceed local needs, they are passed along to fulfill the needs elsewhere."[1]

Fast offering are used exclusively to feed the hungry, clothe the naked, and relieve the suffering of others. Giving a generous fast offering not only benefits the recipient, it rewards those who give. Marion G. Romney admonished: "Be liberal in your giving, that you yourselves may grow. Don't give just for the benefit of the poor, but give for your own welfare. Give enough so that you can give yourself

---

1. Joseph B. Wirthlin, "The Law of the Fast," *Ensign,* May 2001, 73.

into the kingdom of God through consecrating of your means and your time."[2]

And, "If we will double our fast offerings we shall increase our prosperity, both spiritually and temporally. This the Lord has promised, this has been the record."[3]

Most of us live an abundant life—that is a blessing given to us by our Heavenly Father. Fast offerings enable us to share our blessing with others. It is a physical manifestation of our gratitude for all that the Lord has given us.

In the Hymn "Because I Have Been Given Much" we sing:

Because I have been given much, I too must give;
Because of thy great bounty Lord, each day I live
I shall divide my gifts from thee,
        with ev'ry brother that I see
Who has the need of help from me.

Because I have been sheltered, fed by thy good care,
I cannot see another's lack and I not share
My glowing fire, my loaf of bread,
        my roof's safe shelter overhead,
That he too may be comforted.[4]

If you were to give your fast offering directly to the Lord, would He be pleased with your generosity?

2. Marion G. Romney, "The Blessings of the Fast," *Ensign,* July 1982, 4.
3. Quoted by Henry D. Taylor, "The Law of the Fast," *Ensign,* November 1974, 14.
4. *Hymns of The Church of Jesus Christ of Latter-Day Saints,* (Salt Lake City: The Church of Jesus Christ of Latter-day Saints, 1985), no. 219.

Chapter 31

Compassion and Forgiveness

Your Personal Truth

- Is there someone you know who deserves your compassion and forgiveness?
- Do you carry around grudges or make judgmental statements about others?
- Is forgiveness a suggestion or a requirement for salvation?
- Do you have a need to be forgiven?

God forgives. The message is repeated throughout the scriptures. One of the fundamental principles of the gospel is forgiveness. The Savior's mortal mission was one of compassion and forgiveness. And, He expects us to do likewise: "of you it is required to forgive all men" (D&C 64:10). Otherwise, "for he that forgiveth not his brother his trespasses standeth condemned before the Lord; for there remaineth in him the greater sin" (D&C 64:9). To teach us about the principle of forgiveness, Jesus related the parable of the unmerciful servant.

A certain king had a servant who owed him ten thousand talents. Because the servant could not pay the debt, the lord ordered him, his wife and children, and all his possessions to be sold and payment made. The servant pleaded "Lord, have patience with me, and I will pay thee all." Moved with compassion, the king released the servant and forgave him the debt. The same servant went out and found a fellow servant who owed him one hundred pence and took him by the throat. The servant pleaded, "Have patience with me, and I will pay thee all." But he would not, and had him cast into prison.

When the lord heard what was done, he called the servant he forgave and said, "O thou wicked servant, I forgave thee all thy debt, because thou desiredst me: Shouldest not thou also have had compassion on thy fellow servant, even as I had pity on thee? And his lord

131

was wroth, and delivered him to the tormentors, till he should pay all that was due unto him. So likewise shall my heavenly Father do also unto you, if ye from your hearts forgive not every one his brother their trespasses" (see Matthew 18:23-35).

Unless we have compassion, which is charity or the pure love of Christ, we cannot be saved—but "whoso is found possessed of it at the last day, it shall be well with him" (Moroni 7:47). President Spencer W. Kimball wrote of the peril of unforgiveness: "He who will not forgive others breaks down the bridge over which he himself must travel."[1]

We are indebted to the Lord for all our possessions, our family and friends, and life itself. There will come a time, after this life, when we all stand before Him, unable to repay the debt that will admit us into exaltation. Then we will plead, "Lord, have patience with me." Imagine if His response is, "Verily, verily, I say unto you, my servants, that inasmuch as you have forgiven one another your trespasses, even so I, the Lord, forgive you" (D&C 82:1).

Does your present record of compassion towards others make you eligible to receive the forgiveness you seek from the Lord?

---

1. Spencer W. Kimball, *The Miracle of Forgiveness* (Salt Lake City: Bookcraft, 1969), 269.

Compassion and Forgiveness

Dares to Improve Your Life

- I dare you to pray for compassion, that you will learn to forgive and love your enemies.

- I dare you to say you are sorry and make amends to anyone you have misjudged or harbored a grudge against.

- I dare you to write down five good things you see in everyone who has offended you.

- I dare you to write a letter of forgiveness to someone who has hurt or offended you.

There is a Spanish tale of a father and son who had become estranged after years of bitter strife. One day the son ran away. Discovering his son missing, the father was brokenhearted and set off to find him. Weeks of search became months to no avail. Finally, in a last desperate act, the father placed an ad in the local newspaper. The ad read: "Dear Paco, Meet me in front of the bell tower in the plaza at noon on Saturday. All is forgiven. I love you. Your Father." That Saturday 800 Pacos—men and boys—showed up in the plaza, looking for forgiveness and love from their fathers.[1]

Anger, resentment, grudges, hate, and vengeance are heavy burdens to carry. They crush our spirit and cut us off from the Lord. "For verily, verily I say unto you, he that hath the spirit of contention is not of me, but is of the devil, who is the father of contention, and he stirreth up the hearts of men to contend with anger, one with another" (3 Nephi 11:29).

Conversely, Alexander Pope wrote: "To err is human, to forgive divine."[2] Turning the other cheek, giving others the benefit of the doubt, overlooking fault, letting go, showing compassion, forgiving

---

1. Anonymous folk tale.
2. Alexander Pope, *An Essay on Criticism,* 2:1711.

and forgetting are all divine attributes that invite the Spirit of Christ into our lives. Jesus said: "Blessed are the peacemakers: for they shall be called the children of God" (Matthew 5:9).

Learning to forgive and forget is a divine attribute we all must aspire to obtain. President Gordon B. Hinckley has said, "A spirit of forgiveness and an attitude of love and compassion toward those who may have wronged us is of the very essence of the gospel of Jesus Christ. Each of us has need of this spirit. The whole world has need of it. The Lord taught it. He exemplified it as none other has exemplified it."[3]

The source of forgiveness is the pure love of Christ.

Throughout His life the Savior suffered injustice, betrayal by those closest to Him, and both physical and spiritual pain. While His broken and bleeding body hung on the cross, still taunted by enemies, He pled, "Father, forgive them; for they know not what they do" (Luke 23:34). None of us will ever be called upon to forgive so generously; to show such mercy and love.

Who among us does not wish to be accepted and unconditionally loved?

Is there a Paco in your life who needs your forgiveness and love?

---

3. Gordon B. Hinckley, "Of You It Is Required to Forgive," *Ensign,* June 1991, 2.

Chapter 32

Patriarchal Blessings

Your Personal Truth

- Do you know what your mission in life is?
- Have you ever wished that Heavenly Father would give you personal direction for your life?
- Could studying your patriarchal blessing inspire you to live a better life?
- Do you use your patriarchal blessing for direction in setting goals, for motivation and comfort?

"I am glad Beethoven found his way into music, Rembrandt into art, Michelangelo into sculpturing, and President David O. McKay into teaching. To find your proper niche and do well at it can bless you, yours, and your fellowmen . . ." explained President Ezra Taft Benson. "Ponder and pray about it; study closely your patriarchal blessing . . ."[1]

We live in a day of prophets and patriarchs—in a day when God speaks directly to us through His inspired servants. We each have the right to receive an "inspired and prophetic statement of [our] life's mission together with blessings, cautions, and admonitions"[2] from our Father in Heaven, through one of His chosen and ordained patriarchs.

When we receive our patriarchal blessing, we are told many of the blessings God has in store for us in this life and throughout eternity,

---

1. Ezra Taft Benson, *The Teachings of Ezra Taft Benson* (Salt Lake City: Bookcraft, 1988), 484–485.
2. Ezra Taft Benson, *Come, Listen to a Prophet's Voice* (Salt Lake City: Deseret Book Co., 1990), 16.

if we will strive to live true and faithful lives. It is our Heavenly Father's personal counsel to us individually.

Often, spiritual gifts and special talents are revealed. It may contain warnings and instructions to help us successfully fulfill our mission in mortality. If we will study it regularly, it can be a source of strength and motivation.

It also reveals our lineage, the ancestral line we descended from in the House of Israel, through which we become joint heirs to the blessing the Lord promised to Abraham, Isaac, and Jacob.

Our patriarchal blessing provides a glimpse of our divine nature and our eternal possibilities. Elder LeGrand Richards stated: "If we understand where we came from, why we are here, and where we are going, then we are more likely to reach the desired port. That is really the purpose of a patriarchal blessing, to be able to interpret and reveal to us, through the inspiration of the Almighty, why we are here and what is expected of us."[3]

Each of us should desire to receive our patriarchal blessing. President Gordon B. Hinckley counseled: "I hope that we are encouraging those who are mature enough to understand the importance of a patriarchal blessing to receive one. I count my patriarchal blessing as one of the great sacred things of my life. A patriarchal blessing is a unique and sacred and personal and wonderful thing given to every member of this Church who lives worthy of it . . . What a unique, personal, individual, wonderful thing is a patriarchal blessing spoken by authority of the priesthood and the office and calling of patriarch in the name of the Lord Jesus Christ."[4]

How often do you read and study your personal revelation from Heavenly Father?

---

3. LeGrand Richards, "Patriarchal Blessings," *New Era*, February 1977, 4.
4. Gordon B. Hinckley, "Inspirational Thoughts," *Ensign*, August 1997, 3.

Patriarchal Blessings

Dares to Improve Your Life

- If you have not yet received your patriarchal blessing, I dare you to prepare yourself spiritually to receive it.

- I dare you to make a list of the blessings promised in your patriarchal blessing and then list the corresponding instructions for obtaining them.

- Each Sunday for a month, I dare you to study your patriarchal blessing, searching for clues about your mission in life.

- I dare you to make a list of warnings and admonitions revealed in your patriarchal blessing.

A patriarchal blessing has been likened to the Liahona given to Lehi by the Lord. As we journey through mortality, it provides direction to help us avoid hazards and chart a course that will lead us back to our heavenly home. Like the Liahona, it is a gift from God that works "according to [our] faith in God" (Alma 37:40). It should be read and reread, again and again, over a lifetime. Its message must be pondered and prayed about, throughout our life, and the Lord will "give unto the faithful line upon line, precept upon precept" (D&C 98:12) advice, comfort, motivation, warning, and direction to aid us in our journey through mortality.

Our patriarchal blessing is personal revelation from our Heavenly Father that should be cherished and followed. President Thomas S. Monson has explained: "Your patriarchal blessing is yours and yours alone. It may be brief or lengthy, simple or profound. Length and language do not a patriarchal blessing make. It is the Spirit that conveys the true meaning. Your blessing is not to be folded neatly and tucked away. It is not to be framed or published. Rather, it is to be read. It is to be loved. It is to be followed. Your patriarchal blessing will see you through the darkest night. It will guide you through life's dangers."[1]

A patriarchal blessing is invaluable in setting goals. Weaknesses and strengths are pointed out, along with warnings and admonitions. It reveals the special gifts and talents the Lord has blessed us with.

"Do you think for a moment that Heavenly Father would have sent one of His children to this earth by accident, without the possibility of a significant work to perform? You were preserved to come to the earth in this time for a special purpose," taught Elder H. Burke Peterson. "Not just a few of you, but all of you. There are things for each of you to do that no one else can do as well as you."[2] If we will faithfully and prayerfully study our patriarchal blessing, we will gain a glimpse of our divine potential and our eternal possibilities, so we can accomplish our mission in life.

President Ezra Taft Benson instructed, "Jesus knows that His kingdom will triumph, and He wants you to triumph with it. He knows in advance every strategy the enemy will use against you and the kingdom. He knows your weaknesses and He knows your strengths. By personal revelation you may discover some of your strengths through a careful and prayerful study of your patriarchal blessing. In prayer you can ask Him to reveal to you your weaknesses so that you can amend your life."[3]

What is keeping you from discovering your mission in life?

1. Thomas S. Monson, "Your Patriarchal Blessing: A Liahona of Light," *Ensign,* November 1986, 66.
2. H. Burke Peterson, "Your Life Has a Purpose," *New Era,* May 1979, 4-5.
3. Ezra Taft Benson, *The Teachings of Ezra Taft Benson* (Salt Lake City: Bookcraft, 1988), 214.

Chapter 33

Put It to the Test

```
Your Personal Truth

• Do you appreciate the fact that the Book of Mormon was
  written especially with you in mind?
• Are you neglecting your spiritual progress by not studying
  the Book of Mormon?
• Would you like to improve your personal relationship with
  Jesus Christ?
• Do you want to draw nearer to God and His influence?
```

"Is there not something deep in our hearts that longs to draw nearer to God, to be more like Him in our daily walk, to feel His presence with us constantly? If so, then the Book of Mormon will help us do so more than any other book,"[1] promised President Ezra Taft Benson. The prophet Joseph Smith said: "a man would get nearer to God by abiding by its precepts, than by an other book."[2]

God is the ultimate author of the Book of Mormon. It stands as a witness of Him, and His Son, the Savior Jesus Christ. In the Book of Mormon we hear the voice of God introducing His "beloved Son, Jesus Christ," we hear the Savior speak directly to the people: "Behold, I am Jesus Christ, whom the prophets testified shall come into the world" (3 Nephi 11:7-10), and we have an account of His atonement.

Although the Book of Mormon is the record of a fallen people, it is much more than a history book. In fact, Jacob writes that his

---

1. Ezra Taft Benson, "The Keystone of Our Religion," *Ensign*, January 1992, 2.
2. Joseph Smith, *History of the Church of Jesus Christ of Latter-day Saints*, 7 vols., introduction and notes by B.H. Roberts (Salt Lake City: The Church of Jesus Christ of Latter-day Saints, 1932-1951), 4:461.

brother Nephi commanded "that I should not touch, save it were lightly, concerning the history of this people" (Jacob 1:2). Instead, inspired record keepers compiled the "most precious" narratives, testimonies and doctrine for the benefit of our generation.

Nephi wrote: "the Lord God promised unto me that these things which I write shall be kept and preserved, and handed down unto my seed, from generation to generation" (2 Nephi 25:21). Moroni, the last writer, actually saw our day and wrote: "Behold, the Lord hath shown unto me great and marvelous things concerning that which must shortly come, at that day when these things shall come forth among you. Behold, I speak unto you as if ye were present, and yet ye are not. But behold, Jesus Christ hath shown you unto me, and I know your doing" (Mormon 8:34-35). The Lord himself has told us, "the Book of Mormon and the holy scriptures are given of me for your instruction" (D&C 33:16).

We have been admonished, commanded, directed, encouraged, instructed, prompted, taught, and warned to read and study the Book of Mormon. That "Every Latter-day Saint should make the study of this book a lifetime pursuit. Otherwise he is placing his soul in jeopardy and neglecting that which could give spiritual and intellectual unity to his whole life."[3] Yet there are many who have not heeded the counsel. Have you? If not, why?

President Gordon B. Hinckley has said: "I hope that every man and woman and boy and girl has read the Book of Mormon. I hope you have pondered its contents. I hope you have prayed about it if you have any doubts concerning it. I hope you will read it again, and again, and again."[4]

Are you "placing your soul in jeopardy" by not studying the Book of Mormon?

---

3. Ezra Taft Benson citing Marion G. Romney in *Conference Report,* April 1975, 97.

4. Gordon B. Hinckley, *Stand a Little Taller,* (Salt Lake City: Eagle Gate, 2001), 282.

Put It to the Test

Dares to Improve Your Life

- No matter how many times you have read it, I dare you to start reading the Book of Mormon again—today.
- I dare you to read Moroni 10:4-5 and put the challenge to the test.
- Each day for a month, I dare you to read the Book of Mormon with the intent of learning more about the Savior.
- I dare you to record your testimony of the Book of Mormon in a journal, or share it with another person.

"May I tell you of a great adventure? As I traveled to a weekend assignment, I took with me an unusual book which was my constant companion. I could lay it down only to sleep, eat, and change trains. It fascinated me, captivated me, and held me spellbound with its irresistible charm and engaging interest. I have read it many times. As I finished it, I closed the book and sat back, absorbed as I relived its contents . . . It is a story of courage, faith, and fortitude, of perseverance, sacrifice, and super-human accomplishments, of intrigue, of revenge, of disaster, of war, murder, and rapine, of idolatry, and of cannibalism, of miracles, visions, and manifestations, of prophecies and their fulfillment. I found in it life at its best and at its worst, in ever-changing patterns. I hardly recovered from one great crisis until another engulfed me."[1]

Spencer W. Kimball spoke often of his great love of the Book of Mormon. He was fascinated by its stories, teachings, and declaration of the divinity of our Savior, Jesus Christ.

---

1. Spencer W. Kimball, *Conference Report,* April 1963, Afternoon Meeting, 62.

Latter-day Saints have been given this priceless gift, but tragically, many have not gained a testimony of its power to transform their lives. President Ezra Taft Benson has said: "It is not just that the Book of Mormon teaches us truth, though it indeed does that. It is not just that the Book of Mormon bears testimony of Christ, though it indeed does that, too. But there is something more. There is a power in the book, which will begin to flow into your lives the moment you begin a serious study of the book. You will find greater power to resist temptation. You will find the power to avoid deception. You will find the power to stay on the strait and narrow path. The scriptures are called 'the words of life' (D&C 84:85), and nowhere is that more true than it is of the Book of Mormon. When you begin to hunger and thirst after those words, you will find life in greater and greater abundance."[2]

Every Latter-day Saint should be familiar with Moroni's challenge: "And when ye shall receive these things, I would exhort you that ye would ask God, the Eternal Father, in the name of Christ, if these things are not true; and if ye shall ask with a sincere heart, with real intent, having faith in Christ, he will manifest the truth of it unto you, by the power of the Holy Ghost. And by the power of the Holy Ghost ye may know the truth of all things" (Moroni 10:4-5).

Have you personally put Moroni's challenge to the test?

---

2. Ezra Taft Benson, "The Keystone of Our Religion," *Ensign,* January 1992, 2.

Chapter 34

Record-Keeping People

Your Personal Truth

- Is journal writing an important part of your life?
- Is keeping a journal a suggestion or a commandment?
- Can writing down your feelings help you to better understand and process them?
- Can journal writing bring you closer to God?

Latter-day Saints are a record-keeping people. We have a rich heritage of journal writers. "The Church Archives contain diaries kept by Joseph Smith, Oliver Cowdery, Brigham Young, Wilford Woodruff, Parley and Orson Pratt, John Taylor, Heber C. Kimball, Eliza R. Snow, Heber J. Grant, Joseph F. Smith, David O. McKay, and scores of other Church leaders."[1] Thousands of diaries kept by ordinary Church members are preserved in Utah libraries.

A journal is for the benefit of the writer and those who may one day read it. President Spencer W. Kimball spoke often of the importance of keeping a journal and set a perfect example by doing so. In an entry from July 1951, he wrote: "I would like for my posterity to remember me and to know that I have tried so hard to measure up and to live worthy." It is inspiring to read the personal account of a person who struggled, like we all do, and triumphed.

Many have read and studied the words of a young Jewish girl named Anne Frank, who died in the Holocaust. On Saturday, 20 June 1942, Frank wrote: "It's an odd idea for someone like me to keep a diary; not only because I have never done so before, but because it seems to me that neither I—nor for that matter anyone else—will be

---

1. William G. Hartley, "Diary and Journal Ideas," *New Era*, March 1977, 39.

interested in the unbosomings of a thirteen-year-old schoolgirl. Still, what does that matter? I want to write, but more than that, I want to bring out all kinds of things that lie buried deep in my heart."[2]

The detailed descriptions of wall colors, drapery fabric, furnishings and placement of objects in the Beehive House contained in the journal of Brigham Young's daughter Clarissa proved invaluable when the Church began restoration of the home.

Some have traced their family history from journals, experiencing the turning of "the hearts of the fathers to the children, and the hearts of the children to their fathers" (Malachi 4:6).

A journal can be a refuge from worldly stress. In the solitude of writing we hear our own voice clearer and are free to honestly express our range of emotions, from pain and loneliness to joy and love. It is a place to record spiritual experiences that we can later draw strength from in times of struggle. Spencer W. Kimball said: "Those who keep a personal journal are more likely to keep the Lord in remembrance in their daily lives."[3]

Writing a journal can help us see clearer what we want to achieve in life and chart our progress. Helen Keller, who was both blind and deaf, wrote: "I don't want to live in a hand-me-down world of others' experiences. I want to write about me, my discoveries, my fears, my feelings, about me."

Do you value your experiences and testimony enough to write them down?

---

2. Anne Frank, *Anne Frank: The Diary of a Young Girl* (Prentice Hall, 1993), 2.
3. "President Kimball Speaks Out on Personal Journals," *New Era*, December 1980, 27.

Record-Keeping People

Dares to Improve Your Life

- I dare you to obey the commandment to keep a journal.
- I dare you to dedicate a specific time each day or week to write in your journal.
- I dare you to commit to writing a journal for one month.
- I dare you to record your testimony in your journal.

Since the beginning of mortality, God has commanded His people to keep records. Adam kept "a book of remembrance" (Moses 6:5), God directed Moses to "write the things I shall speak" (Moses 1:40), and when Jesus visited the Nephites, He directed them to "bring forth the record which ye have kept" for Him to inspect. Discovering they omitted important events, "[He] commanded that it should be written" and chastened them to be more thorough (see 3 Nephi 23:6-13).

Latter-day prophets have reminded us that Heavenly Father expects us to keep a journal. President Spencer W. Kimball said: "Get a notebook . . . a journal that will last through all time . . . Begin today and write in it your goings and comings, your deepest thoughts, your achievements and your failures, your associations and your triumphs, your impressions and your testimonies. Remember, the Savior chastised those who failed to record important events."[1]

And from President Gordon B. Hinckley, "May I suggest that you write, that you keep journals, that you express your thoughts on paper. . . . You will bless the lives of many—your families and others—now and in the years to come."[2]

---

1. Spencer W. Kimball, "The Angels May Quote from It," *New Era*, October 1975, 5.
2. Gordon B. Hinckley,"If Thou Art Faithful," *Ensign*, November 1984, 91.

A journal is your personal history. It should document the events of your life. President Joseph Fielding Smith instructed: "every important event in our lives should be placed in a record, by us individually . . . If you have accomplished something worth while during the day, put it down."[3] Write your testimony as it grows. Tell of your struggles and how you overcame them.

Brother M. Gawain Wells, a psychologist with Brigham Young University's Comprehensive Clinic, expressed interest in the effects of family record-keeping on mental health: "Keeping a journal gives you a chance to let some whisperings trickle through from your own spirit, as well as from the Spirit of the Lord . . . It helps you get closer in touch with the Lord's time frame, when you can read your own intimate history over a period of months rather than days. Patterns emerge, and you can see clearly the hand of the Lord in your life. You can see how he has helped you and answered some prayers by events, not revelations, in a quiet way that escaped you in the press of circumstances."[4]

Dedicate a specific time each day or week to write in your journal, perhaps on Sunday, and commit to do it. In the beginning it may be difficult, but over time the benefits will become so apparent that you will look forward to writing.

President Spencer W. Kimball said: "Every person should keep a journal and every person can keep a journal. It should be an enlightening one and should bring great blessings and happiness to the families. If there is anyone here who isn't doing so, will you repent today and change—change your life?"[5]

Do you need to "repent today" and start keeping a journal?

---

3. Joseph Fielding Smith, *Doctrines of Salvation,* 3 vols., edited by Bruce R. McConkie, (Salt Lake City; Bookcraft, 1954-1956), 2:204.
4. Quoted from Janet Brigham, "Discover Yourself: Keep a Journal," *Ensign,* Dec. 1980, 57.
5. Spencer W. Kimball, "Let Us Move Forward and Upward," *Ensign,* May 1979, 84.

Chapter 35

Good Deed Doers

```
╭─────────────────────────────────────────────╮
│              Your Personal Truth              │
│  • Are you a regular and consistent doer of good deeds?  │
│  • Can you increase your personal happiness by giving of  │
│    yourself to others?                        │
│  • Do you think of others as your equal?      │
│  • What good have you done in the world today? │
╰─────────────────────────────────────────────╯
```

"I am of the opinion that my life belongs to the community," said writer George Bernard Shaw, "and as long as I live it is my privilege to do for it whatever I can. I want to be thoroughly used up when I die, for the harder I work, the more I live. Life is not a 'brief candle' to me. It is a sort of splendid torch which I have got hold of for a moment, and I want to make it burn as brightly as possible before handing it on to future generations."[1]

It is a law of motion in physics that for every action, there is an equal and opposite reaction. When we put good out into the world, it comes back to us. It has been said that the happiness you feel is in direct proportion to the love you give. The Golden Rule teaches: Do unto others as you would have them do unto you. Imbedded in each of these teachings is the fact that compassion, love, and genuine concern for humankind are reciprocal gifts.

Christians have an exacting charge to esteem all those they associate with and to look for ways to bless the lives of others. The Lord said, "And let every man esteem his brother as himself, and practice virtue and holiness before me. And again I say unto you, let every man esteem his brother as himself" (D&C 38:24-25). Followers of Jesus Christ must be willing to share their time and means with any-

---

1. George Bernard Shaw, original source unknown.

one, at anytime, who needs their help and attention. They are interested in the sick and afflicted, the elderly, the young, the poor, the lonely, the unrighteous and unwise. They do not judge. Instead they show up and reach out to help those who are struggling. They are good-deed doers.

Members of Christ's church make a covenant to care for one another. The prophet Alma taught: "As ye are desirous to come into the fold of God, and to be called his people, and are willing to bear one another's burdens, that they may be light; yea, and are willing to mourn with those that mourn; yea, and comfort those that stand in need of comfort," (Mosiah 18:8-9). That sacred promise was sealed by baptism, "a testimony that ye have entered into a covenant to serve [God] until you are dead as to the mortal body" (Mosiah 18:13). Our compassion for others and "determination to serve" (D&C 20:37) is manifestation of our commitment to the Lord and His gospel.

Speaking of the blessings of concern for others, President Spencer W. Kimball said: "When we concern ourselves more with others, there is less time to be concerned with ourselves . . . So often, our acts of service consist of simple encouragement or of giving mundane help with mundane tasks, but what glorious consequences can flow from mundane acts and from small but deliberate deeds!"[2]

There is an old Chinese proverb that says, "Thousands of candles can be lighted from a single candle, and the life of the candle will never be shortened. Happiness never ceases by being shared."

Is your life a splendid torch that lights other lives?

---

2. Spencer W. Kimball, "Small Acts of Service," *Ensign,* December 1974, 2.

Good Deed Doers

Dares to Improve Your Life

- This week, I dare you to do something that physically lightens the burden of another person.

- I dare you to give a gift or service to a person who can never repay you, and do it anonymously.

- I dare you to pray for inspiration to know who needs your help and how you can give it.

- Each day for a month, I dare you to do a good deed for someone.

At the conclusion of the visit, the home teacher or visiting teachers repeats these familiar words: "Is there anything we can do to help you? If so, please give us a call." In the days and weeks that follow between monthly visits, how often do you think a person in need picks up the telephone and calls for relief? Some do, it is true, but most will continue to bear their loneliness, pain, distress, fear, discouragement, loss, or other burdens alone or with immediate family. The teachers discharged their duty by asking—or did they?

American editor and writer Edgar Watson Howe penned these profound words of wisdom: "If a friend is in trouble, don't annoy him by asking if there is anything you can do. Think up something appropriate and do it." As Christians, we have been charged to "lift up the hands which hang down, and the feeble knees;" (Hebrews 12:12) and to "bear one another's burdens, that they may be light;" (Mosiah 18:8). To "lift," "bear" and "light[en]" are physical manifestations of our love and concern. They are much more than offering to assist—they are showing up and doing something that physically helps another.

We lighten another's load by driving them or their children when their car is broken down, by baby-sitting for a couple who desperately need time alone together, by fixing a meal for someone who is ill or burdened with demands on their time or resources, by repairing a roof, raking a yard, shoveling snow from a drive or walkway, picking up a prescription, helping study for a test, taking time to direct someone who is lost, feeding and clothing the homeless, caring enough to see a need and then showing up to fulfill it without being asked. Mahatma Gandhi gave this insightful charge: "Be the change that you want to see in the world."

Stop saying, "If there is anything I can do . . ." and start doing something!

President Gordon B. Hinckley said, "I do not care how old you are, how young you are, whatever. You can lift people and help them. Heaven knows there are so very, very, very many people in this world who need help. Oh, so very, very many."[1]

The Savior's life was one of compassion and concern for mankind. Even in His last mortal hours, while hanging in agony upon the cross, He exhibited loving concern for His mother's welfare, charging His disciple to care for her (see John 19:25-27). Throughout His mortal ministry, Jesus Christ taught by example and issued this charge: "That ye love one another; as I have loved you, that ye also love one another. By this shall all men know that ye are my disciples, if ye have love one to another" (John 13:34-35).

"If a friend is in trouble, don't annoy him by asking if there is anything you can do"—do something!

Does your record of service bear proof of your discipleship of Christ?

---

1. Gordon B. Hinckley, *Stand a Little Taller,* (Salt Lake City: Eagle Gate, 2001), 218.

Chapter 36

Laws of the Land

Your Personal Truth

- In your daily life, do you honor the laws of the land?
- Does obeying the laws of the land have any impact on your integrity and spirituality?
- Are there spiritual blessings in obeying the laws of the land?
- Do you make a distinction between spiritual laws and temporal laws?

During a lesson about "Obeying the Laws of the Land," one couple shared the ongoing debate they have with their children over buckling seatbelts each time they get into the car. "Until one day," said the mother, "one of the children asked me 'Why?' I answered, 'Because it is the law and Latter-day Saints believe in obeying, honoring, and sustaining the laws of the land.'" The couple reported that was the last time the family had a discussion of seatbelt safety.

After ward tithes and offerings had been counted and logged appropriately, a member of the bishopric, followed by the ward clerk, raced to the bank's after hours depository to make the weekly deposit. Invariably, the counselor would have to wait a minute or two for the clerk to arrive and witness the drop. One Sunday, the counselor asked the clerk why, when they left the Church parking lot together, he always arrived a few minutes later. The clerk explained, "I believe in obeying, honoring, and sustaining the law. Therefore, I obey the posted speed limits."

Part of living the gospel is obeying the laws of the land—"We believe in being subject to kings, presidents, rulers, and magistrates, in obeying, honoring, and sustaining the law" (Articles of Faith 12)—whether they are convenient or not.

To some, obeying speed limits, seat belt, bicycle helmet, and hand signal laws seems insignificant in the eternal perspective. Not so. The Lord has said, "All things unto me are spiritual, and not at any time have I given unto you a law which was temporal" (D&C 29:34). Early in the history of the Church the Lord commanded, "Let no man break the laws of the land" (D&C 58:21).

Speaking of the importance of Latter-day Saints obeying the laws of the land, President N. Eldon Tanner stated firmly: "There is no reason or justification for men to disregard or break the law or try to take it into their own hands."[1]

The Pharisees tried to tempt Jesus into an act or statement contrary to Jewish or Roman law. Instead, He set a great example of a law-abiding citizen. Asked if it were lawful to give tribute money unto Caesar, the ruler of the land where Jesus lived, He responded, "Render therefore unto Caesar the things which are Caesar's; and unto God the things that are God's" (Matthew 22:21).

Are you a law-abiding person?

---

1. N. Eldon Tanner, "The Laws of God," *Ensign,* November 1975, 82.

Laws of the Land

Dares to Improve Your Life

- For a month, I dare you to not break any traffic laws, including speeding.
- Starting today, I dare you to always wear your seatbelt.
- I dare you to learn more about your local and national government leaders and vote intelligently in the next election.
- I dare you to write a letter to a government official, expressing gratitude for, or disagreement with, something he or she has done.

The Lord has said, "There is a law, irrevocably decreed in heaven before the foundations of this world, upon which all blessings are predicated—And when we obtain any blessing from God, it is by obedience to that law upon which it is predicated" (D&C 130:20-21).

As with all of God's commands, obedience to the laws of the land earns blessings and freedom. For instance, seatbelt and traffic laws are for our safety. If we always obey the law, we never have to worry about getting caught and charged with a fine or arrest. Submission to the law builds self-discipline and integrity.

President N. Eldon Tanner emphasized the importance of obeying the law in the following statement: "All the laws of God and the laws of nature and the laws of the land are made for the benefit of man, for his comfort, enjoyment, safety, and well-being; and it is up to the individual to learn these laws and to determine whether or not he will enjoy these benefits by obeying the law and by keeping the commandments. My whole purpose . . . is to show that laws exist for our benefit and that to be happy and successful we must obey the laws and regulations pertaining to our activities; and these laws will function either to our joy and well-being or to our detriment and sorrow, according to our actions."[1]

In a plea to earlier Saints to be obedient in all things, James wrote, "For whosoever shall keep the whole law, and yet offend in one point, he is guilty of all" (James 2:10)." We cannot pick and choose which of God's laws we want to obey. We are accountable for all of them, including those we find inconvenient or insignificant. Any attempt to avoid or skirt the laws of the land is dishonest.

Marion G. Romney said, "Latter-day Saints should strictly obey the laws of the government in which they live. By our own declaration of faith we are committed to do so, for we declare to the world that 'we believe in being subject to kings, presidents, rulers, and magistrates, in obeying, honoring, and sustaining the law' (Articles of Faith 12). "[2]

The twelfth Article of Faith is a call to do more than just comply with civic laws. It is also a charge to be good citizens and strengthen our neighborhood, school, community, and nation. We must participate in the political process by becoming knowledgeable about the law and our government leaders, and exercise the right to vote. We must support good leaders, serve where needed, and fight against laws that are against our moral and ethical beliefs.

Obedience to the laws of the land and good citizenship show our appreciation to God for this "choice land" (Ether 2:12).

How would you rate your performance as a citizen?

---

1. N. Eldon Tanner, *Improvement Era,* June 1970, 31.
2. Marion G. Romney, "The Rule of Law," *Ensign,* February 1973, 2.

Chapter 37

The Power of Prayer

> ## Your Personal Truth
> - Do you really believe that God hears and answers your prayers?
> - How often do you pray?
> - Do you ask God for assistance with whatever you need to accomplish or desire to achieve?
> - Are your prayers a conversation or a one-way dialog?

Each day holds an opportunity to speak with God. We have been given privileged access to Him in any place, at any time. All we have to do is ask and He stands ready to answer us with comfort, direction, guidance, knowledge, protection, and strength.

"One of the greatest daily evidences we have of God's great love for each of us is our relationship to Him in our prayers," stated Elder Marvin J. Ashton. "He has invited us to pray constantly. He wants to hear from us. He wants to help us. He wants to guide us. He wants us to be dependent upon him. He wants us to pray always for guidance, strength, and constant protection."[1]

Nephi understood and taught that we must pray often: "if ye would hearken unto the Spirit which teacheth a man to pray ye would know that ye must pray; for the evil spirit teacheth not a man to pray . . . But behold, I say unto you that ye must pray always, and not faint; that ye must not perform any thing unto the Lord save in the first place ye shall pray unto the Father in the name of Christ, that he will consecrate thy performance unto thee, that thy performance may be for the welfare of thy soul" (2 Nephi 32:8-9).

---

1. Marvin J. Ashton, *Ye Are My Friends* (Salt Lake City: Deseret Book Co., 1972), 36-37.

In our day, President Gordon B. Hinckley has counseled: "Prayer unlocks the powers of heaven in our behalf. Prayer is the great gift which our Eternal Father has given us by which we may approach Him and speak with Him in the name of the Lord Jesus Christ. Be prayerful . . . You need the help of the Lord."[2]

Pray—talk to God. Humbly bare your soul to Him. Tell Him your feelings that you dare not speak aloud. Share with Him your hopes and fears. Pray for forgiveness. Pray for mercy. Pray for your enemies and for those you love. Pray for compassion. Pray for humility, charity, and love. Pray for understanding. Pray to know what to do in life and what not to do. Pray for knowledge of His will and the strength to fulfill it. Pray for comfort. Pray for protection. Pray when your heart is breaking. Pray when you are joyful. Pray with gratitude. Pray with love. Open up your heart and then listen. Listen to what He says.

If we are humble the Lord has promised He will "lead [us] by the hand, and give answer to [our] prayer" (D&C 112:10). Is there any more personal assurance of His love and protection than to be lead by the hand?

We should never underestimate the power of prayer. The gospel of Jesus Christ was restored to the earth after the fervent prayer of a 14-year-old boy. God heard Joseph Smith's prayer and He hears each of our prayers.

Today, have you prayed and put your hand in God's?

2. Gordon B. Hinckley, Pittsburgh Pennsylvania Regional Conference, April 28, 1996.

The Power of Prayer

Dares to Improve Your Life

- I dare you to open up your heart when you speak to Heavenly Father and say what you truly feel.

- I dare you to get down on your knees at least once every day and pray—and when you finish, I dare you to stay on your knees for another 1-3 minutes and just listen.

- I dare you to visualize yourself speaking to Heavenly Father when you pray.

- I dare you to make your prayers more specific: pray for answers to a question, for guidance in a situation, to love an enemy, to forgive an injustice, or for help solving a particular problem—then listen for His response.

A friend extends an invitation to call upon them at anytime; to seek their companionship; to ask and they will answer. Certainly you would respond. Heavenly Father has extended a more generous and consequential invitation: "Draw near unto me and I will draw near unto you; seek me diligently and ye shall find me; ask, and ye shall receive; knock, and it shall be opened unto you" (D&C 88:63). The invitation has been extended—we must make the effort to accept it.

Throughout His mortal ministry Jesus Christ communed constantly with His Father through prayer. Prior to every important decision and in times of suffering He sought His Father's counsel and comfort in prayer. After His baptism, He went into the wilderness and "fasted forty days and forty nights" (Matthew 4:2 and Mark 1:13). Before calling His Twelve Apostles, "he went out into a mountain to pray, and continued all night in prayer to God" (Luke 6:12). In the agony of Gethsemane He prayed to His Father (see Matthew 26:39).

Of the Savior's pattern of prayer, Elder John B. Dickson of the Seventy wrote, "Like us, Jesus Christ, our exemplar and advocate with the Father, was born into this earth life and faced with uncertainties, challenges, and temptations. The Savior taught us by both word and example that we don't have to be alone while in the unfamiliar surroundings of this mortal probation. There is great security in knowing that we can communicate with our Heavenly Father and that He will hear our sincere prayers."[1]

Jesus wanted us to understand the power of prayer. He taught us how to pray (see Matthew 6:9-13 and 3 Nephi 13:6-15). He set an example—one of the most beautiful illustrations of prayer is recorded in 3 Nephi 13, during the Savior's ministry to the Nephites when he "knelt upon the earth and . . . prayed unto the Father" (vs. 15). We read, "and no tongue can speak, neither can there be written by any man, neither can the hearts of men conceive so great and marvelous things as we both saw and heard Jesus speak" (vs. 17) "and he took their little children, one by one, and blessed them, and prayed unto the Father for them. And when he had done this he wept again" (vs. 21, 22). Imagine!

President Gordon B. Hinckley directed, "Believe in prayer. My brothers and sisters, I hope there isn't a man or woman or child here who does not believe in the efficacy of prayer. I remind you that the Church came out of an initial prayer offered by the boy, Joseph Smith . . . The Lord will hear the prayers of faithful people as certainly as He heard the prayers of the boy Joseph. I believe that with all my heart."[2]

"There is no other resource to compare with prayer. To think that each of us may approach our Father in Heaven . . . for individual help and guidance, for strength and faith, is a miracle in and of itself."[3]

Heavenly Father has extended the invitation with a promise: "Ask, and it shall be given you; seek, and ye shall find; knock, and it shall be opened unto you: For every one that asketh receiveth; and he that seeketh findeth; and to him that knocketh it shall be opened" (Matthew 7:7-8).

How have you responded to His invitation?

---

1. John B. Dickson, "'Draw Near unto Me': The Privilege and Power of Prayer," *Ensign*, February 2001, 19
2. Gordon B. Hinckley, "Latter-day Counsel: Selections from Addresses of President Gordon B. Hinckley," *Ensign*, April 2001, 73.
3. Gordon B. Hinckley, "Great Shall Be the Peace of Thy Children," *Ensign*, November 2000, 50.

Chapter 38

Wealth and Consecration

Your Personal Truth

- Do you use your financial resources to live a comfortable life or a luxurious one?

- Is wealth a gift, a right, a blessing, a responsibility, or purely luck?

- Do you consecrate any of your income toward building the kingdom of God? Could you do more?

- Does your wealth distract you from noticing the needs of those around you?

Most of us live in a world of abundance. Never before in history have so many of us luxuriated in such ease and extravagance. Consider the conveniences and comforts we enjoy and even take for granted each day: central heating and air conditioning brings physical comfort to our lives; automobiles and airplanes take us where we need and want to go; telephones allow us to instantly connect with friends and family around the globe; the proliferation of technology brings the world into our living rooms with one flick of the television remote or offers us seemingly limitless information at the touch of a finger on the computer keyboard, and so much more. For many, these blessings bring the desire for more and more. Things once thought extravagances are mistakenly considered necessities.

Moroni saw the prosperity of our day and warned, "Ye adorn yourself with that which hath no life, and yet suffer the hungry, and the needy, and the naked, and the sick and the afflicted to pass by you, and notice them not" (Mormon 8:39). Greed, selfishness and over-indulgence tempt too many to incur financial debt to obtain them, or waste resources that could be used for savings or to help build God's kingdom.

The Lord has told us "all things unto me are spiritual" (D&C 29:34). This includes wealth. Nephi warned, "Wherefore, do not spend money for that which is of no worth, nor your labor for that which cannot satisfy" (2 Nephi 9:51). To develop a more spiritual philosophy of wealth, we must remember that all things belong to the Lord and we have been given sacred stewardship over the blessings He has loaned us (see D&C 104). Elder Joe J. Christensen explained: "Our resources are a stewardship, not our possessions. I am confident that we will literally be called upon to make an accounting before God concerning how we have used them to bless lives and build the kingdom."[1]

A faithful steward will "take of the abundance which [the Lord] have made" and impart of it "unto the needy" (D&C 104:18) and for building up God's kingdom. "Whether our portion is great or small, we can be responsible caretakers as we apply righteous principles."[2]

"Andrew Carnegie, one of this country's great philanthropists, stated his attitude toward wealth as follows: 'This, then, is held to be the duty of the man of wealth: First, to set an example of modesty, unostentatious living, shunning display or extravagance; to provide moderately for the legitimate wants of those dependent upon him; and after doing so to consider all surplus revenues which come to him simply as trust funds, which he is called upon to administer, and strictly bound as a matter of duty to administer in the manner which, in his judgment, is best calculated to produce the most beneficial results for the community—the man of wealth thus becoming the mere trustee and agent for his poorer brethren, bringing to their service his superior wisdom, experience, and ability to administer, doing for them better than they would or could do for themselves.'"[3]

Are you earning spiritual dividends with your wealth?

---

1. Joe J. Christensen, "Greed, Selfishness, and Overindulgence," *Ensign,* May 1999, 11.
2. Visiting Teaching Message: "Living within Our Means," *Ensign,* Feb. 2001, 69.
3. Quoted from Franklin D. Richards, "The Law of Abundance," *Ensign,* June 1971, 45.

Wealth and Consecration

Dares to Improve Your Life

- I dare you to write down your expenditures for a month and determine which are necessities and which are luxuries.

- I dare you to prayerfully consider ways you can use your wealth to build up God's kingdom, and commit to do something towards that end.

- I dare you to determine a luxury you can live without and share the money you save with someone in need.

- I dare you to make a donation or give a gift anonymously to a charitable organization.

"The Lord has blessed us as a people with a prosperity unequaled in times past. The resources that have been placed in our power are good, and necessary to our work here on the earth," said President Spencer W. Kimball. His fear was that many worship the things that prosperity can buy, "spend[ing] most of their time working in the service of a self-image that includes sufficient money, stocks, bonds, investment portfolios, property, credit cards, furnishings, automobiles, and the like to guarantee carnal security throughout, it is hoped, a long and happy life. Forgotten is the fact that our assignment is to use these many resources . . . to build up the kingdom of God—to further the missionary effort and the genealogical and temple work . . . to bless others in every way . . ."[1]

Not long ago a mobile telephone was a luxury, used mostly by workers needing to remain in contact with their employer and clients while away from the office. Today, for many, it is considered a necessity. Siblings that once shared bedrooms have grown into adults whose children each require their own space, furnished with

---

1. Spencer W. Kimball, "The False Gods We Worship," *Ensign*, June 1976, 4-5.

television sets, stereos, and computers. Families are going into debt to acquire another new car, a larger house, or a longer vacation to a more exotic locale. But, how much is enough? Even those who can afford to pay for luxuries without incurring debt must ask, "How much is enough?"

God has made it clear that wealth is a gift given to build His kingdom, and those who misuse it face a penalty. ". . . for it is he that giveth thee power to get wealth, that he may establish his covenant . . . if thou do at all forget the Lord thy God, and walk after other gods, and serve them, and worship them . . . ye shall surely perish" (Deuteronomy 8:18-19).

Many have said: "If I had more wealth, I would donate more to the Church, build a hospital, establish a charitable fund, support missionaries financially, or give in other ways." But how much wealth is needed before we have enough to share?

President Brigham Young said: "When this people are prepared to properly use the riches of this world for the building up of the Kingdom of God, He is ready and willing to bestow them upon us. I like to see men get rich by their industry, prudence, management and economy, and then devote it to the building up of the Kingdom of God upon the earth."[2]

Imagine a world in which men accumulate wealth as a means of blessing the lives of others. Where we "love [our] neighbor as [our] self" (see Leviticus 19:18, Matthew 19:19) enough to share the prosperity that God has blessed us with.

How much wealth is necessary before you begin sharing what you have?

---

2. Brigham Young, *Journal Discourses,* 26 vols. (London: Latter-day Saints' Book Depot, 1854-1866), vol. 2, 114-15.

Chapter 39

Labels

Your Personal Truth

- Do you place worldly labels on the individuals you meet?
- Do you judge people by what others think?
- Do you try to see others as God sees them?
- Is there someone you have falsely labeled that could use your "benefit of the doubt"?

We see someone for the first time and label them cute, beautiful, handsome, thin, fat, tall, short, stylish, fit, and the list goes on and on. We are introduced to someone new and the first questions are often "What do you do for a living?" "What is your major in college?" "Where did you go to school?" "How many children do you have?" and an appropriate label is attached. Our assessments may seem innocent, used to discover common interests, but too often they become a personal judgment that is not a true reflection of the individual. Labels distract us from seeing a real person with feelings, hopes, fears, and dreams.

This fact is illustrated in a story told by Elder Thomas S. Monson. He was visiting The National Gallery in London, England, one of the greatest art museums in the world. "The gallery proudly proclaims its Rembrandt Room and Constable Corner and urges all to take the tour of Turner's masterpieces. Visitors come from every corner of the earth. They depart uplifted and inspired. During a visit to the National Gallery, I was surprised to see displayed in a most prominent location magnificent portraits and landscapes which featured the name of no artist. Then I noticed a large placard which provided this explanation: 'This exhibition is drawn from the large number of paintings that hang in a public but somewhat neglected area of the Gallery: the lower floor. The exhibition is intended to encourage visitors to look at the paintings without being too worried about who painted them. In several instances, we do not precisely know. The information on labels on paintings can often affect, half-unconsciously, our estimate of them; and here labeling has been deliberately subordinate in the hope that visitors will read only after they have looked and made their own assessment of each work.'"[1]

Like labels on paintings, too often we judge others by their appearance, or label them by the world's esteem of their job or wealth. But that is not how God sees us; and it is not how He wants us to see our brothers and sisters. "The Lord seeth not as man seeth; for man looketh on the outward appearance, but the Lord looketh on the heart" (1 Samuel 16:7). Heavenly Father and Jesus Christ look on the heart, and they want us to learn to do the same.

We will begin to change the way we see others if we first attach the label "child of God," remembering that He loves all of us regardless of social status, appearance, or circumstance. The Lord suffered "that *all* men might repent and come unto him" (D&C 18:11), not just those who land a great job or dress in the latest style.

President Brigham Young remarked, "It is not by words, particularly, nor by actions, that men will be judged in the great day of the Lord; but, in connection with words and actions, the sentiments and intentions of the hearts will be taken, and by these will men be judged."[2]

How do you wish to be labeled?

---

1. Thomas S. Monson, "Labels," *Ensign,* September 2000, 2.
2. Brigham Young, *Journal of Discourses, op. cit.,* vol. 8, 10.

Labels

Dares to Improve Your Life

- For a day, I dare you to try to imagine yourself in the shoes of those you come in contact with.
- I dare you to select a specific person whom you judged harshly, and pray for the ability to see him as God sees him.
- Each time you are tempted to make a negative remark about someone, I dare you to find something positive to say instead.
- I dare you to select one person of whom you have been judgmental and make a list of 25 good things about him.

Years ago there was a popular song that challenged: "Walk a mile in my shoes, before you abuse, criticize and accuse, walk a mile in my shoes."[1] How differently we might judge or act toward one another if we exchanged lives for even a day.

But I cannot walk in your shoes, and you will never walk in mine. I can only imagine what your day, week, year or lifetime has been and you can only guess at mine. I do not know what combination of experiences influenced your choices and behavior, just as you do not know mine. In a letter to the Romans the apostle Paul counseled, "Let us not therefore judge one another any more: but judge this rather, that no man put a stumblingblock or an occasion to fall in his brother's way" (Romans 14:13).

Instead of looking for ways to trip up others, we should be reaching out with compassion and love to help one another step up, step forward, step over any obstacles that impede progress. Mother Theresa put it beautifully: "If you judge people, you have not time to love them."

---

1. Joe South, "Walk a Mile in My Shoes," Lowery Music Company, Inc.

The vicious act of faultfinding is nothing more than an attempt to see ourselves as superior. It distorts our perception of others and ourselves and weakens our ability to see our own shortcomings. N. Eldon Tanner pointed out, "If there be one place in life where the attitude of the agnostic is acceptable, it is in this matter of judging. It is the courage to say, 'I don't know. I am waiting for further evidence. I must hear both sides of the question.'"[2]

While here in mortality, even the Lord refrained from making final judgments, "for I came not to judge the world, but to save the world" (John 12:47). His was a life of compassion and love.

Each of us makes mistakes. Each of us wants, and expects, others to forgive our shortcomings and understand our motivations. But do we extend the same mercy? The Lord has said, "Blessed are the merciful: for they shall obtain mercy" (Matthew 5:7). There would be much less hatred, envy, arrogance, bitterness and strife in the world if we each replaced judgment with mercy and love.

President Gordon B. Hinckley has asked "that each of us turn from the negativism that so permeates our society and look for the remarkable good among those with whom we associate, that we speak of one another's virtues more than we speak of one another's faults, that optimism replace pessimism, that our faith exceed our fears."[3]

William Shakespeare wrote: "The quality of mercy is not strain'd, It droppeth as the gentle rain from heaven, Upon the place beneath. It is twice blest: It blesseth him that gives and him that takes."[4]

Will you replace judgment with love?

---

2. N. Eldon Tanner, "Judge Not, That Ye Be Not Judged," *Ensign,* July 1972, 34.
3. Gordon B. Hinckley, "The Continuing Pursuit of Truth," *Ensign,* April 1986, 2.
4. William Shakespeare, *The Merchant of Venice,* Act iv. Sc. 1.

Chapter 40

Prioritized Time

Your Personal Truth

- What do you value most in life?
- What percentage of your time each day do you devote to the people and activities you claim are most important to you?
- How much time each day do you devote to your personal spiritual progress?
- Is your life a living testimony of what you value most?

Every choice we make expresses a preference. Some prefer classical music to rock and roll, sporting events to art museums, reading books over watching television. The sum of these preferences makes a statement about who we are and what is important to us.

"We give our lives to that which we give our time," Elder William R. Bradford has stated, ". . . while here in mortality we are subject to time. We also have agency and may do what we will with our time. Let me repeat: We give our lives to that which we give our time."[1]

Sometimes the desire for what we prefer becomes so strong that our judgment of what is truly important is impaired. The Adversary tries to entice us into making choices that will waste precious time on worldly endeavors instead of devoting that time toward eternal pursuits. "While wholesome pleasure results from much we do that is good, it is not our prime purpose for being on earth," admonished Elder Richard G. Scott. "Seek to know and do the will of the Lord, not just what is convenient or what makes life easy."[2]

---

1. William R. Bradford, "Unclutter Your Life," *Ensign*, May 1992, 27.
2. Richard G. Scott, "First Things First," *Ensign*, May 2001, 9.

It is vitally important to our eternal progression that we put what is most important first in our lives. Elder Neal A. Maxwell said, "An inventory of how we spend our disposable time will tell us where our treasure is"[3] (see Matthew 6:19-21).

Are we so caught up in the details and activities of our lives that we do not make time for that which is most important to us: the things and relationships that have lasting and eternal value?

Jesus gave a beautiful lesson on priorities when He called upon His good friends, sisters Martha and Mary. While Mary sat at Jesus' feet and feasted upon His word, "Martha was cumbered about much serving . . ." The preparations for her guest had become more important than enjoying His company. She asked, "Lord, dost thou not care that my sister hath left me to serve alone? bid her therefore that she help me." Jesus' gentle response was, "Martha, Martha, thou art careful and troubled about many things: But one thing is needful: and Mary hath chosen that good part, which shall not be taken away from her" (Luke 10:38-42). While Martha busied herself preparing the meal, she was missing the actual feast.

The Greek emperor and philosopher Marcus Aurelius wrote, "The true measure of a man is measured by the objects he pursues."

What have you spent your time pursuing today?

---

3. Neal A. Maxwell, *Notwithstanding My Weakness* (Salt Lake City: Deseret Book Co., 1981), 116-117.

Prioritized Time

Dares to Improve Your Life

- I dare you to make a list of what is most important to you.
- I dare you to evaluate how you use your time each day.
- I dare you to rearrange your time according to what you value most and set all other priorities after.
- I dare you to become aware of your misused or wasted time and then prayerfully work to re-appropriate it.

Time is one of life's wondrous riches. How we spend it is a living testament of what is most precious to us. John Ruskin wrote: "Value is the life-giving power of anything; cost, the quantity of labor required to produce it; price, the quantity of labor which its possessor will take in exchange for it."[1]

The people and things we devote our time and resources to are evidence of what is of supreme importance to us.

On a mount near the Sea of Galilee, Jesus taught this eternal truth: "Lay not up for yourselves treasures upon earth, where moth and rust doth corrupt, and where thieves break through and steal: But lay up for yourselves treasures in heaven, where neither moth nor rust doth corrupt, and where thieves do not break through nor steal: For where your treasure is, there will your heart be also" (Matthew 6:19-21).

Who would not agree that the scriptures are of great worth? But to the person who never reads or studies them, what value do they really hold? What value do we place on service to our fellow men? On relationships with our family and friends? On prayer? Elder Joseph S. Geddes said, "I believe that actions speak so much louder than words

---

1. John Ruskin, *Munera Pulveris,* (1862), chapter 1.

that we can scarcely hear what we say when placed in comparison with what we do."[2]

Periodically we need to inventory how our time is spent. Elder William R. Bradford has suggested, "We need to examine all the ways we use our time: our work, our ambitions, our affiliations, and the habits that drive our actions. As we make such a study, we will be able to better understand what we should really be spending our time doing."

Jacob, a Book of Mormon prophet, testified, "But wo unto him that has the law given, yea, that has all the commandments of God [the fullness of the gospel], like unto us, and that transgresseth them, and that wasteth the days of his probation, for awful is his state!" (2 Nephi 9:27.) Time and effort paid for things that have little or no value toward our eternal progress are wasted resources. Elder Richard G. Scott adds, "An axiom we all understand is that you get what you pay for. That is true for spiritual matters as well."[3]

William Shakespeare proclaimed, "This above all: to thine own self be true." Truth exacts an honest inventory of how time and resources are spent.

What have you bought with your time today?

---

2. Joseph S. Geddes, *Conference Report*, April 1914, Second Overflow Meeting, 62.
3. Richard G. Scott, "First Things First," *Ensign*, May 2001, 9.

Chapter 41

Knowing God

Your Personal Truth

- What will you give to know God?
- Is a personal relationship with Heavenly Father an important aspect of the gospel?
- Does having a personal relationship with God influence the choices you make in life?
- When you pray, do you really believe you are literally conversing with your Father in Heaven?

A group of young adults were given a writing assignment to describe their father for someone who had never met him, then list five reasons they love their father and five reasons they know he loves them. Next, with Heavenly Father in mind, they were instructed to write their answers to the same questions. Most answered the questions without too much difficulty. The challenge is to develop a relationship with our Heavenly Father that is as real and intimate as the relationship we have with our earthly father.

Each of us has a responsibility to increase our understanding of the nature of God and to come to know Him personally. It is the primary belief of our religion: "We believe in God, the Eternal Father . . ." (Articles of Faith 1:1.) Joseph Smith taught, "It is the first principle of the gospel to know for a certainty the character of God, and to know that we may converse with him as one man converses with another, and that he was once a man like us . . ."[1]

Our understanding of God's nature and our relationship to Him affects everything we think and do. It affects the way we perceive

---

1. Joseph Smith, *Discourses of the Prophet Joseph Smith,* compiled by Alma P. Burton (Salt Lake City: Deseret Book Co., 1977), 32.

ourselves—our self-worth and our understanding of our divine potential. It affects our ability to pray with sincerity, our desire to pray often, and our faith that we are heard. It affects our Church activity and the amount and attitude of service we render. It affects our values, our integrity, and the way we respond to trials. It affects our scripture study and obedience to commandments. When we understand who God is, His plan of salvation, and our importance to Him, our lives take on meaning and conviction. When we truly come to know that we are literally the offspring of God (Acts 17:28-29) with the potential for exaltation (see Moses 1:39), we will want to live our life in accordance with His commandments (see 1 John 2:3-6).

Each of us must build and strengthen our personal relationship with Heavenly Father. President Gordon B. Hinckley has testified: "I believe without equivocation or reservation in God, the Eternal Father. He is my Father, the Father of my spirit, and the Father of the spirits of all men. He is the great Creator, the Ruler of the Universe. He directed the creation of this earth on which we live. In His image man was created. He is personal. He is real. He is individual. He has 'a body of flesh and bones as tangible as man's' (D&C 130:22)."[2] We too, must come to the knowledge of these truths.

The relationship we have with our earthly father is built over time spent together talking, listening, learning from him, and through obedience. It is the same with our Heavenly Father. We build a personal relationship with him over time spent in praying, listening, studying the scriptures, serving Him, and through obedience to His will.

It is vital to the success of our mission in mortality that we gain a personal relationship with our Heavenly Father. President James E. Faust affirms, "Having such a relationship can unchain the divinity within us, and nothing can make a greater difference in our lives as we come to know and understand our divine relationship with God . . ."[3]

Have you unchained the divinity within yourself through your relationship with God?

---

2. Gordon B. Hinckley, "The Father, Son, and Holy Ghost," *Ensign,* March 1998, 2.
3. James E. Faust, "That We Might Know Thee," *Ensign,* January 1999, 2.

Knowing God

Dares to Improve Your Life

- I dare you to spend a day (a week, a month, a lifetime) searching the scriptures to gain knowledge of your Father in Heaven.

- I dare you to kneel down and pray, with the desire to build a relationship with your Heavenly Father.

- I dare you to study the book of Abraham with the intent of knowing more about God.

- I dare you to make your prayers two-way conversations with Heavenly Father—pour out your heart to Him and take time to listen for His counsel.

"What is the greatest need in the world?" was the question once posed to a group of missionaries. President James E. Faust relates that, "One wisely responded, 'Is not the greatest need in all of the world for every person to have a personal, ongoing, daily, continuing relationship with Deity?'"[1]

Many claim to know God. Latter-day Saints frequently talk and sing about our relationship to God. In primary we learn to sing with conviction "I Am a Child of God." The Proclamation on the Family states: "All human beings—male and female—are created in the image of God. Each is a beloved spirit son or daughter of heavenly parents . . ." The First Article of Faith affirms: "We believe in God, the Eternal Father . . ." Many claim to know God, but actions speak so much louder than words.

When we know God—when we have a personal testimony of His existence, His love for us, and His wondrous plan of salvation—we want to obey Him. Our obedience to His commandments is an expression of gratitude and love for all He has given us. Elder Bernard P. Brockbank, Assistant to the Council of the Twelve, wrote: "There is a difference in believing or knowing there is a God and in knowing God.

---

1. James E. Faust, "That We Might Know Thee," *Ensign,* January 1999, 2.

When we claim that we know God, it bears great responsibility, and an apostle has given us information to check our knowledge of God. The apostle John said: 'And hereby we do know that we know him, if we keep his commandments. He that saith, I know him, and keepeth not his commandments, is a liar, and the truth is not in him. But whoso keepeth his word, in him verily is the love of God perfected: hereby know we that we are in him. He that saith he abideth in him ought himself also so to walk, even as he walked.' (1 John 2:3-6.)"[1]

Heavenly Father loves each of His children. His goal is for us to be like Him (Moses 1:39). The First Presidency and Quorum of the Twelve has said: "Your Heavenly Father wants your life to be joyful and lead you back into His presence. The decisions you make now will determine much of what will follow during your life and throughout eternity. Because the Lord loves you, He has given you commandments and the words of the prophets to guide you on your journey."[2]

Our relationship with Heavenly Father is fostered and strengthened by studying the words of ancient and modern prophets to learn His will, and in striving to obey His commandments, giving service, and prayer. Our ability to call on Him at any time is one of the great evidences of our Father in Heaven's love for us. President Gordon B. Hinckley has said: "Prayer is the great gift which our Eternal Father has given us by which we may approach Him and speak with Him in the name of the Lord Jesus Christ."[3]

President Harold B. Lee stated: "I would charge you to say again and again to yourselves, . . . 'I am [a son or daughter] of God' and by so doing begin today to live closer to those ideals which will make your life happier and more fruitful because of an awakened realization of who you are."[4]

Do you believe—or do you know that you are a child of God?

---

1. Bernard P. Brockbank, "Knowing God," *Ensign*, July 1972, 121.
2. *For The Strength of Youth, Fulfilling Our Duty to God* pamphlet, The Church of Jesus Christ of Latter-day Saints, 2001, 2.
3. Gordon B. Hinckley, *Pittsburgh Pennsylvania Regional Conference,* April 28, 1996.
4. Harold B. Lee, "Understanding Who We Are Brings Self-Respect," *Ensign,* January 1974, 2.

Chapter 42

Listening Skills

Your Personal Truth

- Are you a good listener?
- Do you need to sharpen your listening skills?
- Do you demonstrate your love and respect by listening to those you care about?
- Can you ease the burdens of others by listening to them?

A young girl was late arriving home from school. Her mother began to scold the girl, but stopped and asked, "Why are you so late?" "I had to help another girl—she was in trouble," replied the daughter. "What did you do to help her?" "Oh, I sat down and listened to her."

Listening demonstrates respect and understanding. Giving our time, focusing our attention and listening with an open mind and heart, free of judgment and unsolicited advice, is an act of sacrifice and an expression of love.

Sister Sharon L. Larson, Second Counselor in the Young Women General Presidency, has said that loving is a vital part of listening. She learned that lesson from her father, and explained, "I know what listening really is, because I have had the blessed experience. I used to farm with my dad. I didn't always enjoy it, but when lunchtime came we'd sit in the shade of the tall poplar trees, eat our lunch, and talk. My dad didn't use this as a golden teaching moment to lay down the law and straighten out his daughter. We just talked—about anything and everything. This was the time I could ask questions. I felt so safe I could even ask questions that might provoke him."[1]

---

1. Sharon L Larson, "Fear Not: For They That Be With Us Are More," *Ensign,* November 2001, 67.

It has been said that God created us with two ears and one mouth because listening demands twice the skills of talking. For most people, listening is a skill that requires constant sharpening. A good listener stops whatever else he is doing and focuses full attention on the person speaking. He makes eye contact and will often lean toward the speaker or nod his head to show he is paying attention. True listening is not a discussion or a conversation. A good listener hears what is being said without making judgment. A good listener is self-disciplined—not waiting to tell his own story; but silently concentrates on what the other person is saying. He does not offer advice, unless specifically asked, and does not try to solve the problem for the other person.

The art of listening can be improved by consciously trying to listen twice as long as you speak. It can sometimes be helpful to rephrase what has been said or ask a few questions for clarification.

Listening demonstrates that we respect and value the person speaking. By listening, we learn. In a revelation given to Joseph Smith, the Lord taught, "be still and know that I am God" (D&C 101:16). The principle is also true for our fellowman—if we will "be still" and listen, we will come to know the individual.

Listening builds trust between individuals and fosters a safe place for loved ones to open up and share the feelings of their hearts. Listening is a powerful tool for lifting the spirit of both the speaker and the listener. Author and philosopher Henry David Thoreau wrote: "What means the fact—which is so common, so universal—that some soul that has lost all hope for itself can inspire in another listening soul an infinite confidence in it, even while it is expressing its despair?"[2]

Who did you make time to listen to today?

---

2. Henry David Thoreau, Letter to Lucy Brown dated January 24, 1843, in *The Writings of Henry David Thoreau* (Houghton Mifflin, 1906), vol. 6, 44.

Listening Skills

Dares to Improve Your Life

- When you pray, I dare you to listen for answers twice as long as you speak.

- I dare you to search the scriptures for references to listening and being still.

- Throughout the day, I dare you to consciously take notice of the quiet promptings of the Spirit—write them down as they come and then act on them.

- Each day, I dare you to make time to be still and listen to what God has to say to you.

"The first duty of love is to listen," wrote Paul Tillich. Making time to meditate, focus our attention, and listen with an open mind and heart is an expression of love for our Heavenly Father. Listening demonstrates respect, understanding, faith, and obedience.

Listening is an essential part of our success in mortality. The Savior frequently taught, "He that hath ears to hear, let him hear" (Matthew 11:15; see also Matthew 13:9, Mark 4:23, and Luke 8:8) and warned that those who do not listen "shall be cut off" (D&C 1:14). While those who listen and believe have the promise of "everlasting life" (John 5:24).

Listening for the voice of the Spirit is a skill that requires constant sharpening. Elder Boyd K. Packer once shared that for many years he and his son used a short-wave radio to talk with people in distant parts of the world. "I could hear static and interference and catch a word or two, or sometimes several voices at once. Yet [my son] understood, for he has trained himself to tune out the interference. It is difficult to separate from the confusion of life that quiet voice of inspiration. Unless you attune yourself, you will miss it."[i]

---

1. Boyd K. Packer, "Prayers and Answers," *Ensign,* November 1979, 19.

We must remove ourselves from worldly distractions, focus our attention and be quiet so we can hear. "It is a small voice," stated Elder Joseph B. Wirthlin. "It whispers, not shouts. And so you must be very quiet inside. That is why you may wisely fast when you want to listen. And that is why you will listen best when you feel, 'Father, thy will, not mine, be done.' You will have a feeling of 'I want what you want.' Then, the still small voice will seem as if it pierces you. It may make your bones to quake. More often it will make your heart burn within you, again softly, but with a burning which will lift and reassure."[2]

When we pray, the quality of our listening can be improved by consciously trying to listen twice as long as we speak. The more we listen, the more sensitive we become to the divine impressions that come to us daily. The more we listen and obey the promptings given, the more often the still, small voice of the Spirit will speak to us. By listening, we learn: "be still and know that I am God" (Psalms 46:10 and D&C 101:16).

"The Lord is speaking to you!" taught Elder Graham W. Doxey, of the Seventy. "But with the deafening decibels of today's environment, all too often we fail to hear him. I remember as a youth having the experience of being in company with an older man who had lost much of his hearing ability. He had no hearing aid and was continually asking that we speak louder so that he could be part of the conversation. He would say, 'Talk louder; speak up; I can't hear you.'. . . On religious matters, too many of us are saying, "What did you say? Speak up; I can't hear you." And when [Heavenly Father] doesn't shout back . . . we are inclined to think he doesn't listen, doesn't care about us. Some even conclude there is no God. The questions are not "Does God live? Does God love me? Does God speak to me?" The critical question is, "Are you listening to him?"'[3]

Have you listened to God today?

---

2. Joseph B. Wirthlin, *Finding Peace in Our Lives* (Salt Lake City: Deseret Book Co., 1995), 31.

3. Graham W. Doxey, "The Voice Is Still Small," *Ensign,* November 1991, 25.

Chapter 43

Blessings of the Sabbath

Your Personal Truth

- Do you consider Sunday a holy day or a holiday?
- Do you know the purpose of the Sabbath day?
- What does it mean to keep the Sabbath day holy?
- On Sunday, do you ever finish up projects from work or school, watch non-uplifting television programs, make purchases, play too hard, labor to cook elaborate meals, clean and straighten your home, wash the car, read worldly material?

Since the creation of the earth, one day each week has been set apart by commandment from God for rest, worship and drawing closer to Him and His son, Jesus Christ, and for serving others. He established the pattern from the beginning: "And on the seventh day God ended his work which he had made; and he rested on the seventh day from all his work which he had made. And God blessed the seventh day, and sanctified it: because that in it he had rested from all his work which God created and made" (Genesis 2:2-3).

He reemphasized its sanctity in the fourth of the Ten Commandments: "Remember the sabbath day, to keep it holy" (Exodus 20:8) and explained, "Six days shalt thou labour, and do all thy work: But the seventh day is the sabbath of the Lord thy God: in it thou shalt not do any work" (Exodus 20:9-10).

In our dispensation, through the Prophet Joseph Smith, the Lord decreed: "this is a day appointed unto you to rest from your labors, and to pay thy devotions unto the Most High" by attending church, partaking of the sacrament, and resting from our labors (D&C 59:9-13).

Beyond going to church and partaking of the sacrament and resting from our labors, what are appropriate Sunday activities?

In 1993, the First Presidency offered the following counsel: "We should refrain from shopping on the Sabbath and participating in other commercial and sporting activities that now commonly desecrate the Sabbath. We urge all Latter-day Saints to set this holy day apart from activities of the world and consecrate themselves by entering into a spirit of worship, thanksgiving, service, and family-centered activities appropriate to the Sabbath. As Church members endeavor to make their Sabbath activities compatible with the intent and Spirit of the Lord, their lives will be filled with joy and peace."[1]

Throughout the centuries, few commandments have been repeated more frequently than the divine law of the Sabbath. President Ezra Taft Benson said: "Ancient prophets of God have proclaimed it, and presidents of the Church and other General Authorities have repeatedly emphasized that it be kept holy. Lay Christians and men of goodwill throughout Christendom have spoken approvingly of its place and value in the lives of men, women, and children. No Latter-day Saint need stumble or be in doubt as to his duty in reference to this divine law."[2]

Are all your Sabbath day activities in keeping with the holiness of the Lord's day?

---

1. "Message from the First Presidency," *Ensign,* January 1993, 80.
2. Ezra Taft Benson, "Keeping the Sabbath Day Holy," *Ensign,* May 1971, 4.

Blessings of the Sabbath

Dares to Improve Your Life

- I dare you to make a list of the things you did last Sunday and evaluate your performance in keeping the Sabbath holy.
- I dare you to physically prepare for the Sabbath by completing all chores and other labors on Saturday that cannot wait until Monday.
- I dare you to dedicate the next Sabbath day to God and fill it with activities that bring you closer to Him.
- I dare you to make the Sabbath day a holy day.

The Sabbath day is the Lord's gift of time to us. He knows our bodies and minds need time to rest and rejuvenate. Each week we have been given a day free from physical labor in which we can refresh our minds and spirits, to develop spiritually and draw closer to Heavenly Father and Jesus Christ. The Sabbath should be a day of joy and peace that we look forward to.

The Lord has promised temporal and spiritual blessing to those who observe the Sabbath as a holy day. In ancient times, He promised rain in due season, that the land would yield her increase, safety, peace in the land, protection from enemies, and that He would multiply the obedient and establish His covenant with them (see Leviticus 26:2-9).

Do we not need rain in due season and peace in the land today? Do we not want the Lord to multiply us and establish His covenant with us? All of these guaranteed blessings apply to us today.

In revelation given to the prophet Joseph Smith, the Lord promises our "joy may be full" (D&C 59:13) and that "the fulness of the earth is [ours]" (D&C 59:16).

In modern times, President Joseph Fielding Smith said: "It has been demonstrated many times by those who have forsaken the seventh day for business and have given it to the service of the Lord as he has required, that they have prospered. They testify that they have been more abundantly blessed in their temporal affairs as well as in spiritual needs."[1]

The Sabbath is an appropriate time for us to look after our fellowman. Many people are lonely, sick, in need of encouragement or a listening ear. The Sabbath can be a time for us to succor their needs. By blessing the lives of others, our own lives are richly blessed.

Honest and conscientious observance of the Sabbath is a manifestation of our love and respect for Heavenly Father and Jesus Christ. Elder Mark E. Petersen of the Quorum of the Twelve said: "We can readily see that observance of the Sabbath is an indication of the depth of our conversion. Our observance or nonobservance of the Sabbath is an unerring measure of our attitude toward the Lord personally and toward his suffering in Gethsemane, his death on the cross, and his resurrection from the dead. It is a sign of whether we are Christians in very deed, or whether our conversion is so shallow that commemoration of his atoning sacrifice means little or nothing to us."[2]

What does your observance of the Sabbath day say about your attitude toward God?

1. Joseph Fielding Smith, *Answers to Gospel Questions,* (Salt Lake City: Deseret Book Co., 1957-1966), 1:103.
2. Mark E. Petersen, "The Sabbath Day," *Ensign,* May 1975, 49.

Chapter 44

Think Positive

Your Personal Truth

- Does your attitude towards life affect how happy you are?
- Is attitude important in determining your behavior?
- What challenges do you have right now that might be easier if you developed a positive attitude about them?
- Do your negative thoughts undermine your potential?

Abraham Lincoln wisely said: "Most folks are about as happy as they make up their minds to be."

We may not have control over our circumstances, but we do determine our attitude toward them. No situation or person can force a response upon us—we decide to react negatively or act positively. Shakespeare wrote, "There is nothing either good or bad, but thinking makes it so."

Our attitude is so powerful that it can influence our behavior. In some instances, our attitudes can even affect the outcome of a situation. There is an ancient proverb that says: "A misty morning does not signify a cloudy day." This truth was illustrated in the Book of Mormon story of Nephi obtaining the brass plates.

In First Nephi we read of Lehi and his family fleeing Jerusalem. They were more than three days journey into the wilderness when Lehi received revelation from God, commanding that his sons return to Jerusalem and obtain the brass plates in Laban's possession. Laman and Lemuel murmured that the task was too difficult, but Nephi replied: "I will go and do the things which the Lord hath commanded, for I know that the Lord giveth no commandments unto the children of men, save he shall prepare a way for them that they may accomplish the thing which he commandeth them" (1 Nephi 3:7).

No matter how difficult the task before him, Nephi determined to follow instructions with a positive attitude.

When the first and second attempts to obtain the plates failed, Laman and Lemuel murmured against their brother, their father and the Lord. Nephi, however, remained positive. He did not allow circumstances or other people to determine his attitude. Instead, he placed his trust in the Lord and in so doing, was able to complete the assignment his earthly father and Heavenly Father had given him.

Elder Marvin J. Ashton has counseled: "We must be more concerned with what we do with what happens to us than what happens to us."[1] By developing a positive outlook on life, one that is rooted in faith and trust that the Lord will not require more of us than we can handle, daily life becomes a happier experience.

Author William James wrote: "The greatest discovery of my generation is that a human being can alter his life by altering his attitudes of mind." Our happiness is not dependent upon what happens to us or upon the people we come in contact with. Our happiness comes from within us.

Today, did you expect your happiness to come as a reaction to people and circumstances, or did you take responsibility for your own happiness?

---

1. Marvin J. Ashton, "Who's Losing?" *Ensign,* Nov. 1974, 41.

Think Positive

Dares to Improve Your Life

- I dare you to do one difficult thing today that will make you happier tomorrow.

- I dare you to write a gratitude list and post it—near your computer screen, on the dashboard of your car, on a mirror—where it will be seen when your day becomes stressful.

- I dare you to read the scriptures each morning and notice the change in your attitude.

- The next time you feel unhappy, overwhelmed, angry or rejected, I dare you to get down on your knees and tell the Lord ten (work up to one hundred) things you are grateful for.

"A man's life is what his thoughts make of it," wrote the great Roman Emperor Marcus Aurelius. Our attitudes have such a strong influence over our actions and the type of person we are that Solomon proclaimed: "For as he thinketh in his heart, so is he" (Proverbs 23:7).

"Each of us is the architect of his own fate and he is unfortunate indeed who will try to build himself without realizing that he grows from within, not without," said the prophet David O. McKay. "Thoughts make us what we are . . . Thoughts lift your soul heavenward, or drag you toward hell."[1]

An extraordinary example of man's ability to choose his attitude is found in Viktor Frankl's book *Man's Search for Meaning*. In it he writes: "We who lived in concentration camps can remember the men who walked through the huts comforting others, giving away their last piece of bread. They may have been few in number, but they offer

---

1. *Secrets of a Happy Life,* quoted from Elder William J. Critchlow, Jr., *Conference Report,* April 1963, Afternoon Meeting, 32.

sufficient proof that everything can be taken away from a man but one thing: the last of the human freedoms—to choose one's attitude in any given set of circumstances, to choose one's own way."

Negativity undermines our potential and must be overcome. If you feel gloomy, President Gordon B. Hinckley has suggested: "Lift your eyes. Stand on your feet. Say a few words of appreciation and love to the Lord. Be positive. Think of what great things are occurring as the Lord brings to pass His eternal purposes."[2]

Our lives are shaped by our attitude toward our circumstances. Playwright George Bernard Shaw wrote: "People are always blaming their circumstances for what they are. I don't believe in circumstances. The people who get on in this world are the people who get up and look for the circumstances they want, and, if they can't find them, make them."[3]

It is critical that we learn to create situations that will uplift and strengthen our resolve to remain positive in the direst of circumstances. Fortification can be found in prayer and meditation, reading the scriptures, church publications, and other inspiring material, listening to beautiful music, serving others, smiling, laughing, counting our blessings, taking pleasure in the beauty all around us. Ultimately, our happiness is an outgrowth of striving daily to live gospel principles.

"Two men look out through the same bars: One sees the mud, and one the stars"[4] Life was not just meant to be a test of our endurance—it was also meant to be enjoyed!

When you look upon your day, do you see the mud or do you look toward the stars?

---

2. "Excerpts from Recent Addresses of President Gordon B. Hinckley," *Ensign,* August 1996, 60.
3. *Mrs. Warren's Profession,* in *Plays by George Bernard Shaw,* (New York: New American Library, 1960), 82.
4. Frederick Langbridge, *A Cluster of Quiet Thoughts,* cited in The Oxford Dictionary of Quotations, 2nd edition., (London: Oxford Univ. Press, 1966), 310.

Chapter 45

Movie Pass

Your Personal Truth

- How do you judge the message of the movies you watch?
- Does viewing even one objectionable movie affect you?
- Do the films you watch invite or reject the Spirit of Christ?
- If a film has a good message, does it matter that it contains immoral scenes or vulgar language?

Would you rifle through your kitchen trash hoping to find something good to eat? Would you search the dumpster behind your favorite restaurant looking for a good meal? Of course not! Then why would you watch a movie with unwholesome content?

Rotten movies are damaging to the soul and impossible to purge from your mind. Too often we allow ourselves to get caught in the trap of rationalization; trying to devise a plausible explanation for our acts that may not be in keeping with what we know to be morally correct. Rationalization is, at its core, self-deception.

"Our mind," said H. Burke Peterson, "which is like a tremendous reservoir itself, is capable of taking in whatever it may be fed—good and bad, trash and garbage, as well as righteous thoughts and experiences. As we go through life, we may be exposed to stories, pictures, books, jokes, and language that are filthy and vulgar, or to television shows and movies that are not right for us to see or hear. Our mind will take it all in. It has a capacity to store whatever we will give it. Unfortunately, what our mind takes in, it keeps—sometimes forever. It's a long, long process to cleanse a mind that has been polluted by unclean thoughts."[1]

---

1. H. Burke Peterson, "Purify Our Minds and Spirits," *Ensign,* November 1980, 37.

Some say, "It's only rated R because of the violence" or "There were only a couple of swear words." The fact is, a prophet of God has said: "We counsel you . . . not to pollute your minds with such degrading matter, for the mind through which this filth passes is never the same afterward. Don't see R-rated movies or vulgar videos or participate in any entertainment that is immoral, suggestive, or pornographic."[2] To some the directive is clear, but others will rationalize it as being only a suggestion.

If those guidelines are not distinct enough, the ancient prophet Mormon taught this simple truth that should be applied toward selecting the movies we watch: "all things which are good cometh of God; and that which is evil cometh of the devil" (Moroni 7:12) and that "the Spirit of Christ is given to every man, that he may know good from evil; wherefore, I show unto you the way to judge; for every thing which inviteth to do good, and to persuade to believe in Christ, is sent forth by the power and gift of Christ" (Moroni 7:16). If we will listen, the Spirit will tell us what we should avoid.

Moviemaker Walt Disney said, "Movies can and do have tremendous influence in shaping . . . lives in the realm of entertainment towards the ideals and objectives of normal adulthood."

How are the movies you watch shaping your life's ideals and objectives?

---

2. Ezra Taft Benson, "To the 'Youth of the Noble Birthright,'" *Ensign,* May 1986, 43; and "To the Young Women of the Church," *Ensign,* November 1986, 81.

Movie Pass

Dares to Improve Your Life

- I dare you to refuse to watch any R-rated films in the theater, rental, or on television.
- I dare you to walk out of off-color PG-rated movies.
- I dare you to become more aware of how movies affect your spirit.
- I dare you to voice your approval of uplifting films by writing a letter to the movie theater, producer of the film or to your local newspaper.

It has been said, "You can map your life through your favorite movies, and no two people's maps will be the same." Every scene, every word of dialog, every musical lyric in the movies we see leaves a lasting impression on us. What does your movie map say about you?

"Whatever you read, listen to, or look at has an effect on you," counseled the First Presidency and Quorum of the Twelve. "Therefore, choose only entertainment and media that uplift you. Good entertainment will help you to have good thoughts and make righteous choices. It will allow you to enjoy yourself without losing the Spirit of the Lord."[1]

These inspired leaders further advised: "[Movies] can uplift and inspire you, teach you good and moral principles, and bring you closer to the beauty this world offers. But they can also make what is wrong and evil look normal, exciting, and acceptable . . . Don't attend or participate in any form of entertainment, including concerts, movies, and videocassettes, that is vulgar, immoral, inappropriate, suggestive, or pornographic in any way. Movie ratings do not always

---

1. *For The Strength of Youth, Fulfilling Our Duty to God* pamphlet, The Church of Jesus Christ of Latter-day Saints, 2001, 17.

accurately reflect offensive content. Don't be afraid to walk out of a movie . . . if what's being presented does not meet your Heavenly Father's standards. . . . In short, if you have any question about whether a particular movie . . . is appropriate, don't see it, don't read it, don't participate."[2]

A popular film was billed as having "a significant message," but contained nudity and violence. Another film had beautiful scenery and music, but skillfully woven into the plot of the film was an adulterous relationship. Characters in a PG-rated film touted as "a film for the whole family" repeatedly used the Lord's name in vain and made references to sexual situations. Professional reviews and even friends may encourage us to enjoy certain films that contain material that is offensive to our spirit. We must be on constant guard, using the guidelines given by the prophet, Church leaders, and the Lord himself: "Abstain from all appearance of evil" (1 Thessalonians 5:22).

In a letter to her son John, Susannah Wesley gave this wise counsel that can be used as a guide when we make choices: "Whatever weakens your reason, impairs the tenderness of your conscience, obscures your sight of God, takes from you your thirst for spiritual things or increases the authority of your body over your mind, then that thing to you is evil. By this test you may detect evil no matter how subtly or how plausibly temptation may be presented to you."[3]

What impressions are the movies you watch leaving on your spirit?

---

2. *For The Strength of Youth, Fulfilling Your Duty to God* pamphlet, The Church of Jesus Christ of Latter-day Saints, 1990, 11.
3. Quoted from Thomas S. Monson, comp., *Favorite Quotations from the Collection of Thomas S. Monson* (Salt Lake City: Deseret Book Co., 1985), 90.

Chapter 46

Love is a Verb

Your Personal Truth

- How can you tell that someone loves you?
- How do those you love know that you love them?
- Do you only express your love in words, or is there evidence of your love?
- Is love crucial for salvation?

Doubtless no topic has been written, spoken or sung about more than love. William Shakespeare wrote: "They do not love that do not show their love."[1] Henry Drummond said: "You will find as you look back upon your life that the moments when you have truly loved are the moments when you have done things in the spirit of love." Henry Ward Beecher penned: "Of all earthly music, that which reaches farthest into heaven is the beating of a truly loving heart." And actress Katherine Hepburn put it this way: "Love has nothing to do with what you are expecting to get—only with what you are expecting to give—which is everything." Love is all about giving.

Jesus Christ taught about giving love throughout His mortal life and provided us with the perfect example to follow. The Atonement was the ultimate expression of His and our Heavenly Father's love for us. The apostle John wrote: "God so loved the world, that he gave his only begotten Son" (John 3:16). And Moroni records: "Thou hast loved the world, even unto the laying down of thy life for the world, that thou mightest take it again to prepare a place for the children of men" (Ether 12:33).

Love is the basic principle of the gospel by which we achieve eternal life. When Jesus was asked, "Which is the great command-

---

1. William Shakespeare, *The Two Gentlemen of Verona,* act 1, sc. 2, line 31.

ment?" He responded: "Thou shalt love the Lord thy God with all thy heart, and with all thy soul, and with all thy mind, this is the first and great commandment, and the second is like unto it, thou shalt love thy neighbor as thyself. On these two commandments hang all the law and the prophets" (see Matthew 22:36-40). Through His example, the Savior showed us that love is not simply saying "I love you," but it is the act of giving of oneself for the benefit of another.

The need for giving love is expressed in a story told by Elder Marvin J. Ashton about a friend of his: "Upon returning home from his day's work, this father greeted his boy with a pat on the head and said, 'Son, I want you to know I love you.' The son responded with, 'Oh Dad, I don't want you to love me, I want you to play football with me.'"[2]

Love is a verb—it is an action. Each day we have an opportunity to express love in action: a loving person makes a phone call and listens to someone who needs to be heard; a loving person writes a letter expressing gratitude for an uplifting Sunday school lesson or Sacrament meeting talk; a loving person knows the needs of the individuals he or she home or visit teaches, and actively tries to help; a loving person recognizes a new person at school or church, introduces himself, and invites the person into his home or to an activity; a loving person smiles and says "Hello" to people who cross his path each day; a loving person participates in service projects; a loving person recognizes people as individuals, notices needs, and steps forward to help.

When we return to our Heavenly home and the Savior asks, "Who did you love in my name?" Imagine our sorrow if we cannot look Him in the eye and name names.

To whom have you given love today?

---

2. Marvin J. Ashton, "Love Takes Time," *Ensign,* November 1975, 108.

Love is a Verb

Dares to Improve Your Life

- I dare you to select someone you do not like and make a list of 25 positive things about the person.
- I dare you to pray for God to soften your heart toward someone who has wronged you.
- For a week or month, I dare you to pray daily that God will show you people who need your love and give you the courage to do something to show it.
- For a month, I dare you to express your love daily by doing something for someone else.

Love comforts. Love supports. Love heals. Love nourishes. Love builds. Love serves. Love forgives. Love forgets. Love laughs. Love triumphs. Love transforms.

Above all else, the Lord has commanded us to love—love God, love our neighbor, love ourselves (see Matthew 22:37-39), and love our enemies: "But I say unto you, Love your enemies, bless them that curse you, do good to them that hate you, and pray for them which despitefully use you, and persecute you; That ye may be the children of your Father which is in heaven" (Matthew 5:44-45). Heavenly Father loves all of His children—both the wicked and the righteous—and He has commanded us to do likewise so that we can learn to become like Him.

Speaking of the commandment to love our enemies, President Gordon B. Hinckley has said: "Most of us have not reached that stage of compassion and love and forgiveness. It is not easy. It requires a self-discipline almost greater than we are capable of. But as we try, we come to know that there is a resource of healing, that there is a mighty power of healing in Christ, and that if we are to be his true servants, we must not only exercise that healing power in behalf of others, but, perhaps more important, inwardly."[1]

Love changes hearts: a new counselor was called to serve in a ward bishopric. In the man's previous calling his boisterous nature was an asset. In his new calling, some members of the ward judged him to be irreverent, egotistical and abrasive. One woman determined to learn to love him. In her daily prayer she asked Heavenly Father to soften her heart to recognize the good qualities this man possessed. Over time, she began to notice his gentleness and patience with small children, his enthusiasm for the gospel, and his faithful service to the Lord. The counselor did not change. The woman's heart was changed as she began to see him as the Lord does: "The Lord seeth not as a man seeth . . . but the Lord looketh on the heart" (1 Samuel 16:7). As we learn to let the love of God into our heart, the Spirit teaches us how to love.

Love is not selective; love has no boundaries: "For if ye love them which love you, what reward have ye?" (Matthew 5:46). Love loves the lovable and the not so lovable. "The real test of Christian love," challenged Lowell L. Bennion, "is if you can forgive an enemy who has despitefully used you and hurt you, with or without cause. A Christian can and will love people he doesn't like, that he disagrees with and finds troublesome. To love someone in a Christian spirit, one need only to wish him well and to seek his well-being."[2]

Mother Teresa, a modern-day example of Christlike love, said: "I have found the paradox that if I love until it hurts, then there is no hurt, but only more love."

Who do you need to learn to love?

---

1. Gordon B. Hinckley, *Faith: The Essence of True Religion* (Salt Lake City: Deseret Book Co., 1989), 34.
2. Lowell L. Bennion, *The Best of Lowell L. Bennion: Selected Writings 1928-1988,* edited by Eugene England (Salt Lake City: Deseret Book Co., 1988), 275.

Chapter 47

Be Still and Ponder

A multitude of passages within the scriptures teach that we must "ponder" the things of God. During His mortal life, Jesus frequently withdrew from worldly distractions to a place of solitude where He could commune with God and angels. These quiet moments allowed Him to ponder spiritual matters, identify strengths, and learn how to turn difficulties into advantages.

This same spiritual counseling is available to us. Following Christ's example, we should retire often to a quiet place, free from interruption and distractions, where we can commune with God through silent meditation. In these peaceful moments, we should do as the Savior instructed and "Let the solemnities of eternity rest upon [our] minds" (D&C 43:34) so that the Holy Ghost can teach us all that our Heavenly Father wants us to know and do.

It is through these peaceful deliberations that our eyes are opened to see spiritual matters more clearly. President David O. McKay said, "Meditation is one of the most secret, most sacred doors through which we pass into the presence of the Lord."[1]

---

1. David O. McKay, general conference address, April 1946.

"It was in solitude, pondering and praying, that Jesus made ready to battle Satan face to face and resist and overcome all of his enticements," explained Elder Joseph B. Wirthlin. "It is not in the hurly-burly of everyday life, amid the pressures of business, society, and even family, that we marshal our greatest strengths, discern our hidden resources, and learn how to utilize our God-given powers in order to fight and vanquish the enemy. It is only in solitude, pondering and meditating, that we live in closest relationship with our Lord."[2]

"All my life I have studied and pondered the principles of the gospel and sought to live the laws of the Lord," said the prophet Joseph Fielding Smith. "As a result there has come into my heart a great love for him and for his work and for all those who seek to further his purposes in the earth."[3]

He later wrote, ". . . I sat in my room pondering over the scriptures; and reflecting upon the great atoning sacrifice that was made by the Son of God, for the redemption of the world . . . As I pondered over these things which are written, the eyes of my understanding were opened, and the Spirit of the Lord rested upon me . . ."
(D&C 138:1-2, 11).

If we will make time daily to escape the noise and hurry of our mortal lives for quiet meditation with the Lord, our spirit will be renewed and fortified. Author Bruce Barton wrote: "It would do the world good if every man in it would compel himself occasionally to be absolutely alone. Most of the world's progress has come out of such loneliness."[4]

Have you made time to be alone and listen to the Spirit today?

---

2. Joseph B. Wirthlin, *Finding Peace in Our Lives* (Salt Lake City: Deseret Book Co., 1995), 31.
3. Joseph Fielding Smith, *Conference Report,* October 1971, 6.
4. Bruce Barton, original source unknown.

Be Still and Ponder

Dares to Improve Your Life

- I dare you to schedule time each day to ponder. I dare you to make pondering an integral part of your life—as important as food, water, sleep, and other life-renewing necessities.

- I dare you to take a few minutes at the conclusion of your scripture study to ponder the message of the words you have just read.

- I dare you to ponder upon your mission in life, today.

- I dare you to gain a personal testimony of the power of pondering and then share it with someone else.

Toward the end of the first day of His ministry to the Nephites, Jesus perceived that the people were exhausted physically and mentally. He instructed them to "go ye unto your homes, and ponder upon the things which I have said, and ask of the Father, in my name, that ye may understand, and prepare your minds for the morrow, and I come unto you again" (3 Nephi 17:3).

After our mortal minds have read and studied spiritual matters, the great instruction process begins when we quietly ponder all we have taken in and allow the Spirit to teach us.

"As I have read the scriptures," President Marion G. Romney has said, "I have been challenged by the word ponder, so frequently used in the Book of Mormon. The dictionary says that ponder means 'to weigh mentally, think deeply about, deliberate, meditate . . .' Pondering is, in my feeling, a form of prayer."[1]

Moroni, the great final prophet of the Book of Mormon, admonished us to take advantage of the powerful principle of pondering.

---

1. Marion G. Romney, *Conference Report,* April 1973, 117.

After we have read and studied the scriptures, he wrote, "ponder it out in your hearts" and pray for answers to your questions. To each person who asks God "with sincere heart, with real intent, having faith in Christ," he makes this pledge: "[the Lord] will manifest the truth of it unto you, by the power of the Holy Ghost." He then adds this all-encompassing promise to those seeking answers: "And by the power of the Holy Ghost ye may know the truth of all things" (Moroni 10:3-5). What an extraordinary gift: to "know the truth of all things."

Teaching us to listen for the Spirit, President Ezra Taft Benson once explained: "We hear the words of the Lord most often by feeling. If we are humble and sensitive, the Lord will prompt us through our feelings. That is why spiritual promptings move us on occasion to great joy, sometimes to tears. Many times my emotions have been tender and my feelings very sensitive when touched by the Spirit."[2]

Our Heavenly Father communicates with us through quiet promptings from the Holy Ghost. In order to hear Him, we must make time to reflect, consider, and open our hearts and minds to listen. "I testify," said Elder Joseph B. Wirthlin, "that when the quality of the pondering improves, the quality of prayers and performance improves also."[3]

How would you rate the quality of your pondering?

---

2. Ezra Taft Benson, *Come Unto Christ* (Salt Lake City: Deseret Book Co., 1983), 20.
3. Joseph B. Wirthlin, *Finding Peace in Our Lives* (Salt Lake City: Deseret Book Co., 1995), 31.

Chapter 48

Gossip and Negative Comment

Your Personal Truth

- Does God suggest we refrain from gossip, or has He commanded us not to gossip?
- Is repeating a true story you have heard about another person considered gossip?
- When a friend asks you to not repeat information shared in confidence, do you always honor your promise?
- Do you ever make judgmental comments about others?

"The officers of the court were full of love and understanding, but very serious in their investigation of the charges; those present could lose their membership in The Church of Jesus Christ of Latter-day Saints. The charge was not immorality or apostasy; they were accused of speaking evil of a neighbor. A fine brother had been slandered by those gathered together that evening, accused of the serious charge of immorality. He was completely innocent, but the great damage that had been done by 'those whom he counted as his friends' would not be easily repaired. Who could measure the near destruction of this good soul? Who could measure the impact on the branch, as its fellowship was eroded? And what about the effect on those nonmembers who also became involved? Who could ever undo the evil that had affected hundreds of lives? It had happened so easily. It began with simple words like—'Did you hear . . .?'"[1]

Repeating any negative comment or story, even if factual, serves no purpose but to diminish the character of the person being spoken about. Gossip—telling tales, repeating information shared in confidence, fault finding, spreading rumor, criticizing others, slander,

---

1. Gene R. Cook, "Gossip: Satan's Snare," *Ensign*, January 1981, 27.

speaking evil, judging—is a caustic habit that destroys the person being spoken about, the person speaking, and the person listening. When we gossip, we idly discuss someone else's problems and weaknesses in a vicious attempt to make ourselves seem more significant.

Negative conversations are damaging to our spirit. In the scriptures we learn: "A fool's mouth is his destruction, and his lips are the snare of his soul. The words of a talebearer are as wounds, and they go down into the innermost parts of the belly" (Proverbs 18:7-8). Satan knows how powerfully destructive gossip can be. Prior to the Savior coming to the Americas, "Satan did stir [the people] to do iniquity continually; yea, he did go about spreading rumors and contentions upon all the face of the land, that he might harden the hearts of the people against that which was good and against that which should come" (Helaman 16:22). The Lord has made it clear in His commandment: "Thou shalt not bear false witness against thy neighbor" (Exodus 20:16) that we must refrain from gossip and negative remarks.

Richard L. Evans points out: "To speak abusive words in public, to put libelous statements in print, and to bear false witness in court are offenses that can be traced to their source. But to let words loose on a whisper that sweeps from ear to ear and from lip to lip, and that suggests more than it says, is in some ways among the worst forms of bearing false witness. And because of our receptiveness to gossip and our eagerness to be the first to tell something, we perhaps involve ourselves in the spread of what is false and unfounded oftener than we would wish to admit. "There is nothing that can't be made worse by telling,' said Terence. That which passes out of one mouth passes into a hundred ears."[2]

When someone asks, "Did you hear about. . . ." do you listen, or politely ask them not to share?

---

2. Richard L. Evans, "The Spoken Word," *Ensign,* September 1971, 43.

Gossip and Negative Comment

Dares to Improve Your Life

- Instead of discussing another's mistakes or problems, I dare you to pray for them.
- For today, I dare you to only speak positive and uplifting words.
- For a week, I dare you to refuse to listen to any gossip, fault-finding or negative speaking about another.
- Each time you are tempted to criticize another this week, I dare you to stop and say two good things about them instead.

Remember the parlor game "gossip," where you sat in a circle and whispered a sentence in the ear of the person seated next to you? By the time the sentence made its way around the circle and returned to the originator it had become amusingly garbled. The game powerfully illustrates how quickly a simple line of information can become misconstrued.

When we casually discuss another person's problems or weaknesses, we are engaging in character assassination and gossip. Elder N. Eldon Tanner illustrated the destructive nature of negative words in this story: "We hear a man say to his family and to others, 'I don't see why the bishop does this or that. You would think he would know better.' Here he is judging the bishop without the facts, which, if known to him, would be full justification for the action taken. The man's judgment was not only unrighteous, but it had probably prejudiced his children and caused them to lose respect for the bishop and had weakened their faith."[1]

---

1. N. Eldon Tanner, "Judge Not, That Ye Be Not Judged," *Ensign,* July 1972, 34.

The Lord's people do not speak evil of others. Instead, they follow His command to "Let [their] words tend to edify one another" (D&C 136:24) and "Strengthen your brethren in all your conversations, in all your prayers, in all your exhortations, and in all your doings. And behold, and lo, I am with you to bless you and deliver you forever" (D&C 108:7-8). In a letter to Timothy, Paul counseled all of us, "Be thou an example of the believers, in word, in conversation" (1 Timothy 4:12). Each day is a new opportunity to speak only words that build, restore, commend, encourage, and uplift.

"Two friends found they often criticized another friend when she was not with them. They knew this wasn't good, so they decided to say two good things every time they said one bad thing. It was hard at first, but soon they came to appreciate the qualities of their friend so much that they had no desire to gossip about her."[2]

President Joseph F. Smith taught, "It is so very much better for a person to strive to develop himself by observing all the good points he can find in others, than to strangle the growth of his better self by cherishing a fault-finding, sullen and intermeddling spirit . . . Let it be the aim of the Saints to cultivate the spirit of generosity and good-will, such as was exemplified in the life of Christ . . . Watch constantly for that which is worthy and noble in your fellowman. It makes a person better to see and speak of good in his neighbor; while there is unbounded delight in observing the effect that a few words of appreciation and encouragement have upon men, women, and children with whom we associate. Let those try it who really wish to get the genuine sweets out of life."[3]

The Greek didactic poet Hesiod wrote: "A sparing tongue is the greatest treasure among men."

Do you have a reputation for spreading stories or stopping them?

---

2. Lesson Ideas, Gossip, *Family Home Evening Resource Book,* 191.
3. Joseph F. Smith., *Improvement Era,* March 1903, No. 5.

Chapter 49

Sharing the Gospel

Your Personal Truth

- Why is it important to share the gospel with others?
- Are you afraid to share the gospel? If so, why?
- Do you live your life in such a way that others know what you believe?
- How is sharing the gospel of Jesus Christ an expression of love?

Belgian philosopher Desire-Joseph Mercier wrote, "We must not only give what we have; we must also give what we are." This quote has eternal significance to Latter-day Saints because what we are (followers and messengers of the saving gospel of Jesus Christ) is an outgrowth of what we have to give: the good news that our Heavenly Father loved us so much that He provided a way for us to return to His presence and become like Him. The good news that Jesus Christ loved us so much that He came to earth to show us how to live and provide a way for us to gain salvation and eternal life. The good news of the saving gospel of Jesus Christ: "And this is the gospel, the glad tidings, which the voice out of the heavens bore record unto us—That he came into the world, even Jesus, to be crucified for the world, and to bear the sins of the world, and to sanctify the world, and to cleanse it from all unrighteousness; That through him all might be saved . . ." (D&C 76:40-42).

At baptism we covenant "to stand as witnesses of God at all times and in all things, and in all places that ye may be in," (Mosiah 18:9). The apostle Matthew challenged: "Let your light so shine before men, that they may see your good works, and glorify your Father which is in heaven" (Matthew 5:16). By giving of ourselves and setting an example of how the gospel has blessed our life, we ignite in others the desire to know more, to have what we have.

President Gordon B. Hinckley has said: "Bring people into the Church. Bring them in with love. Bring them in with kindness. Bring them in with the example of your lives. So live the gospel that they will see in you something of wonder and beauty and be encouraged to inquire, study the gospel, and join the Church."[1]

Sharing the gospel is an act of obedience. "The Savior gave us a mandate to teach the gospel to every nation, kindred, tongue, and people,"[2] said President Hinckley. It is also an expression of love—love for our Heavenly Father, love for our Savior Jesus Christ, and love for our fellowman.

When we love someone, we are concerned for their welfare and happiness; we want the best for them. Is there anything that can bring greater joy and happiness into the lives of others than the gospel? Our message, the message of Jesus Christ, is one of salvation and eternal life. If we truly love our neighbor as ourselves, we want to give them what we have and what we are.

"The best way in the world to show our love for our neighbor," said President Heber J. Grant, "is to go forth and proclaim the gospel of the Lord Jesus Christ."[3]

Do you love your neighbors enough to share the gospel with them?

---

1. Gordon B. Hinckley, "Words of the Living Prophet," *Liahona,* June 2001, 34.
2. "Excerpts from Recent Addresses of President Gordon B. Hinckley," *Ensign,* July 1997, 72.
3. Heber J. Grant, *Conference Report,* April 1927, 176.

Sharing the Gospel

Dares to Improve Your Life

- I dare you to recognize the gospel as a wonderful gift and pray for the desire to share it with someone you love.
- I dare you to share a pass-along card with a friend today.
- Each day for a month, I dare you to pray for the opportunity to share your testimony, the inspiration to recognize it, and the courage to do so.
- I dare you to write your testimony in a Book of Mormon and pray for the opportunity to give it to someone.

"Consider that you are invited to a friend's house for breakfast. On the table you see a large pitcher of freshly squeezed orange juice from which your host fills his glass. But he offers you none. Finally, you ask, 'Could I have a glass of orange juice?' He replies, 'Oh, I am sorry. I was afraid you might not like orange juice, and I didn't want to offend you by offering you something you didn't desire.' Now, that sounds absurd," said Elder Robert C. Oaks, "but it is not too different from the way we hesitate to offer up something far sweeter than orange juice."[1]

When we hesitate to share the gospel with those we profess to care about and love, we should stop and assess our fears by asking ourselves: "Am I ashamed of the gospel?" "Do I feel inadequate in sharing my testimony?" "Am I afraid my friends and loved ones will be offended?" Whatever our fear, Satan is behind it, trying to discourage us, trying to thwart the Lord's plan to spread the gospel "throughout every nation, kindred, tongue, and people" (Mosiah 3:20).

The Apostle Paul taught: "For God hath not given us the spirit of fear; but of power, and of love, and of a sound mind. Be not

---

1. Robert C. Oaks, "Sharing the Gospel," *Ensign,* November 2000, 81.

thou therefore ashamed of the testimony of our Lord" (2 Timothy 1:7-8).

In this dispensation, President Gordon B. Hinckley has given similar counsel: "God hath not given you the spirit of fear. That comes from the adversary. The Lord has given you the power of love, and a sound mind; the power of the priesthood, the power of your call, love for the gospel which you teach, for the people you teach, and for the Lord."[2]

The Apostle John taught that love overcomes fear. He wrote: "There is no fear in love; but perfect love casteth out fear . . ." (1 John 4:18). When our desire to share the gospel is based on love, Heavenly Father will help us overcome all fears so we can communicate the truth.

"The intensity of our desire to share the gospel is a great indicator of the extent of our personal conversion," said Elder Dallin H. Oaks. "We must pray for the Lord's help and directions so we can be instruments in His hands for one who is now ready—one He would have us help today."[3]

After the sons of Mosiah experienced a change of heart, they were filled with love for their fellowman and went about sharing the gospel: "They were desirous that salvation should be declared to every creature, for they could not bear that any human soul should perish; yea, even the very thought that any soul should endure endless torment did cause them to quake and tremble" (Mosiah 28:3). When we are filled with love for our Father in Heaven and Jesus Christ, for our family, friends and neighbors, we want them to enjoy the same blessing we can receive through membership in Christ's church.

We must not allow our fear of hurting a friendship stop us from sharing the good news of the gospel of Jesus Christ. President Spencer W. Kimball counseled: "Sometimes we forget that it is better to risk a little ruffling in the relationship of a friend than it is to deprive them of eternal life . . ."[4]

Will you express your love today by sharing the gospel?

---

2. Gordon B. Hinckley, *Stand A Little Taller, Op. Cit.,* 202.
3. Dallin H. Oaks, "Sharing the Gospel," *Ensign,* Nov. 2001, 7.
4. Spencer W. Kimball, *The Teachings of Spencer W. Kimball,* (Salt Lake City: Bookcraft, 1982), 554.

Chapter 50

The Blessings of Challenges

Your Personal Truth

- What blessings have you received as a result of challenges you overcame?
- When faced with painful trials, do you pray for strength, trusting the Lord knows best?
- Have you ever thanked God for unanswered prayers?
- How has a trial strengthened your faith and character?

Quite naturally, we mortals want to know the "Why?" of things, particularly when challenges arise. Some even become depressed, discouraged, or angry, and cry out: "Why me? Why this? Why now?" When viewed through our narrow mortal vision, we may fail to see the blessing in what appears to be an adverse situation. Instead of asking "why," we must learn to face difficulties with courage, faith, and prayer, trusting that the Lord knows best.

The Clark family had a dream to leave their native Scotland to start a new life in the United States. It took several years of hard work and sacrifice, but the parents and their nine children finally saved the money, obtaining passports and reservations on a new ocean liner. The entire family was filled with anticipation and excitement. Just seven days before their departure, the youngest son was bitten by a dog. A doctor stitched up the injury, then hung a yellow sheet of paper on the Clark's front door. Because of the possibility of rabies, they were being quarantined for fourteen days. The family's dream was dashed. They would not be able to make the planned trip to America.

The father, filled with disappointment and anger, stomped to the dock to watch the ship set sail. He shed tears and cursed both his son and God for the family's misfortune. Five days later, tragic news spread throughout Scotland: the mighty Titanic had sunk. The unsinkable ship went down, taking hundreds of lives with it. The Clark family was to have been on that ship. When Mr. Clark heard the news, he hugged his son and thanked God for saving their lives and turning what he had felt was a tragedy into a blessing.[1]

Sometimes Heavenly Father blesses us through unanswered prayers. Singer and songwriter Garth Brooks recorded these profound words:

"Sometimes I thank God for unanswered prayers.

"Remember when you're talkin' to the man upstairs. That just because he may not answer doesn't mean he don't care. Some of God's greatest gifts are unanswered prayers"[2]

When trials loom before us, if we put our trust in the Lord, He has promised us, "I will go before your face. I will be on your right hand and on your left, and my Spirit shall be in your hearts, and mine angels round about you, to bear you up" (D&C 84:88). There is nothing we cannot endure with His assistance.

Instead of asking *why,* we must learn to begin our questions with *what:* "What can I do to improve the situation? What can I learn from this challenge? What wouldst Thou have me do?"

Have you ever thanked God for the blessings you received as a result of overcoming challenges?

---

1. Original Author Unknown.
2. Pat Alger, Larry Bastian, Garth Brooks, "Unanswered Prayers," Major Bob Music and Warner-Chappell Publications.

The Blessings of Challenges

A wise Chinese proverb teaches, "The gem cannot be polished without friction, nor a man perfected without trials."

Mortality is a time of proving ourselves and striving to become more like our Savior, Jesus Christ. In our pre-mortal state, when the Savior said, "We will prove them herewith, to see if they will do all things whatsoever the Lord their God shall command them" (Abraham 3:25), we endorsed the plan and signed on with enthusiasm, knowing this would be a time of testing and growth.

Speaking of mortality, Elder Richard G. Scott said: "It is inter-woven with difficulties, challenges, and burdens . . . Yet these very forces, if squarely faced, provide opportunity for tremendous personal growth and development. The conquering of adversity produces strength of character, forges self-confidence, engenders self-respect, and assures success in righteous endeavor."[1]

Our mortal life could be compared to learning to be a hurdler. "In the 100-meter hurdles race, runners must jump over hurdles placed in their path. The hurdles are not there so that a runner will come to them

---

1. Richard G. Scott, "The Plan for Happiness and Exaltation," *Ensign,* November 1981, 11.

and stop and, discouraged, go back to the starting line. They are not there to make him crash. The beauty and excitement of this race is to jump over the hurdles, to overcome the obstacles. If we understand the importance of the obstacles in our individual lives, we begin to see them in a positive light as true challenges to overcome."[2]

We knew we would face painful trials and disappointments during mortality, but we also knew that we would not be tested beyond our abilities (see D&C 64:20), and that help would be provided. The Lord said: "Look unto me in every thought; doubt not, fear not" (D&C 6:36).

Speaking of the Savior's power to succor us, Elder Neal A. Maxwell said: "As part of His infinite atonement, Jesus knows "according to the flesh" all that through which we pass (see Alma 7:11-12). He has borne the sins, griefs, sorrows,...the pains of every man, woman, and child (see 2 Nephi 9:21). Having been perfected in His empathy, Jesus thus knows how to succor us. We can, therefore, actually do as Peter urged and cast our cares upon the Lord (see 1 Peter 5:7); He is familiar with them, including even the feeling of being forsaken (see Mark 14:50, 15:34). Nothing is beyond His redeeming reach or His encircling empathy. Therefore, we should not complain about our own life's not being a rose garden when we remember who wore the crown of thorns!"[3]

It takes great courage and faith to get on our knees and say, "Not my will, but Thy will be done."

Do you have the strength to ask for help?

---

2. Horacio A. Tenorio, "Teachings of a Loving Father," *Ensign*, May 1990, 79.
3. Neal A. Maxwell, "Overcome . . . Even As I Also Overcame," *Ensign*, May 1987, 70.

Chapter 51

Focus on Family

Your Personal Truth

- What does family mean to you?
- How do your family members know you love them?
- What one thing could you do this week to improve your relationship with your individual family members?
- Do you love your family enough to hold daily prayers, scripture study and weekly family home evening?

As a people, Latter-day Saints value family and understand its vital role in Heavenly Father's eternal plan. In 1995, the First Presidency and Council of the Twelve Apostles issued "The Family: A Proclamation to the World." It declares: "The family is ordained of God" and outlines our responsibilities to strengthen it. The "For the Strength of Youth" pamphlet contains a section devoted to family, which states: "Being part of a family is a blessing. Your family can provide you with companionship and happiness, help you learn correct principles in a loving atmosphere, and help you prepare for eternal life." The phrase "strengthen home and family" was recently added to the Young Women's theme. The very first verse of the Book of Mormon, the keystone of our religion, states: "I, Nephi, having been born of goodly parents, therefore I was taught . . ." (1 Nephi 1:1). And yet, as individuals, do we truly esteem this sacred unit?

Following the counsel of our prophet to hold family prayer, family scripture study, and family home evening is not only proof of our obedience to God's commandments and respect for His marvelous plan, it is also an expression of our love for the individuals that make up our family. It sends a powerful message to our spouse, children, parents, and siblings that they are valued.

"Saul Jose Vargas sat down with his 10-year-old daughter, Maria Isabel, a few weeks ago and began reading from the Book of Mormon. Together they studied passages where Mormon speaks in letters to his son, Moroni. The loving words of a prophet to his scion saddened Saul Jose. He had lost his own father just days earlier and now hungered for spiritual comfort. 'My daughter began to console me, telling me that her grandpa was now in a place where he was no longer suffering,' said Brother Vargas . . . Young Maria Isabel then told her father of the Plan of Salvation, the blessing of the temple and eternal families. A bit surprised, Brother Vargas asked Maria Isabel if she had learned such things in Primary. 'No,' she reminded him, 'we learned about them at home during family home evening.' 'My tears of sadness changed to tears of joy and love,' Brother Vargas said. 'Family home evening has been the foundation of our happy family.'"[1]

Speaking of the power and blessings derived from weekly family home evenings, President Gordon B. Hinckley has said: ". . . I do not hesitate to promise you that both you and your children will become increasingly grateful for the observance of this practice. It was John who declared: 'I have no greater joy than to hear that my children walk in truth.' (3 John 4:1.) This will be your blessing."[2]

In 1915, when President Joseph F. Smith and his counselors introduced the "weekly home evening program" they stated: "If the Saints obey this counsel, we promise that great blessings will result. Love at home and obedience to parents will increase. Faith will develop in the hearts of the youth of Israel, and they will gain power to combat the evil influences and temptations which beset them."[3]

Do you want those blessings for yourself and your family?

---

1. Jason Swensen, "Foundation for a Happy Family: Encouraging Family Home Evening," *LDS Church News,* November 2, 2002.
2. Gordon B. Hinckley, *Teachings of Gordon B. Hinckley* (Salt Lake City: Deseret Book Co., 1997), 211.
3. First Presidency, April 27, 1915, *Improvement Era* 18:733-34.

Focus on Family

Dares to Improve Your Life

- I dare you to hold weekly family home evening for the next month, year, or for the rest of your life.
- I dare you to plan and present a family home evening lesson.
- I dare you to record in your journal how weekly family home evening has blessed your family.
- I dare you to pray for inspiration to know how to improve your family's relationships and follow through on those promptings.

It has been said, "Many people can make a fortune, but very few can build a family."

Through His inspired prophets, our Heavenly Father has given us a miraculous tool for strengthening our home and family: Family Home Evening. Several years ago, Elder George D. Durante conducted a study on the impact of the program. He contacted families who rarely, if ever, held family home evening and challenged them to do so weekly for a period of three months. "I remember one family's experience. When I visited the home to make my original request, the father put his smoking pipe aside. A can of beer was open near the side of his chair. We spoke of several subjects, then I made the request. He accepted, saying that he would faithfully conduct a family home evening each week."

"Winter had nearly turned to spring before I saw the family again. I was greeted by an almost overwhelming welcome. When I asked, 'Did you have a home evening every week for the past three months as you said you would?' The father looked at me intently and said, 'I'm not sure. Most weeks we did, but there was one week we aren't sure if what we did was a family home evening or not.' The mother then said,

'I think we could even count what we did that week.' I said, 'Tell me what you did and we'll see.' The father replied, 'That's the week we went to the temple to be sealed together forever as a family.'"

When Elder Durante asked the father, "What happened to cause this mighty change?' His simple reply was, 'Each week I'd call my family together and we'd have family home evening. I saw the children sitting there close to me and their mother. We all felt so good and so happy. I decided it was time we started changing things. We talked about going to the temple so that we could be together forever. We talked to our home teachers and then to the bishop. After a time the bishop felt we were worthy to go to the temple.'"[1]

"Good homes are not easily created or maintained," said President Gordon B. Hinckley. "They require discipline . . . They require respect for others, that respect which comes best from acceptance of the revealed word of the Lord concerning the purpose of life, of the importance and sacred nature of the family, and recognition of each member of the family as a child of God."[2]

The quality of family home evening is not defined by quantity of individuals. Whatever our circumstances, we can participate in family home evening and will be blessed for doing so. President Spencer W. Kimball and his counselors stated: "It is for families with parents and children, for families with just one parent, and for parents who have no children at home. It is for home evening groups of single adults and for those who live alone or with roommates."[3]

Author George Bernard Shaw wrote: "A happy family is but an earlier heaven."

Do you value your family enough to participate in weekly family home evening?

---

1. George D. Durrant, "Doing Genealogy: Finding That Glorious, Elusive Condition Called 'Balance,'" *Ensign*, April 1985, 18.
2. Gordon B. Hinckley, *Stand A Little Taller*, *Op. Cit.*, 131.
3. *Family Home Evening* manual, 1976, 3.

Chapter 52

Free from the Burden of Sin

> ## Your Personal Truth
>
> - Do you believe the Savior has the power and desire to help you change your life?
> - How can the Atonement help lift, ease and remove your burdens?
> - Can your weaknesses become strengths?
> - How does carrying the burden of unrepentant transgressions impede your progress?

"An old farmer had plowed around a large rock in one of his fields for years. He had broken several plowshares and a cultivator on it and had grown rather morbid about the rock. After breaking another plowshare one day, and remembering all the trouble the rock had caused him through the years, he finally decided to do something about it. When he put the crowbar under the rock, he was surprised to discover that it was only about six inches thick and that he could break it up easily with a sledgehammer. As he was carting the pieces away he had to smile, remembering all the trouble that the rock had caused him over the years and how easy it would have been to get rid of it sooner."[1]

Many carry the weight of sinful habits they feel hopeless to overcome. Others continue to suffer needlessly from unrepented transgressions. When ignored and left unresolved, these oppressive burdens impede progress. They do not understand the good news of the gospel of Jesus Christ—"that he came into the world, even Jesus, to be crucified for the world, and to bear the sins of the world, and to sanctify the world, and to cleanse it from all unrighteousness; that through him all might be saved whom the Father had put into his

---

1. Brian Cavanaugh, "Obstacles? Deal With Them Now," source unknown.

power and made by him" (D&C 76:41-42)—that through the power of the Atonement our spirit can be lifted, our burdens lightened, and the effects of our sins erased.

"What relief! What comfort! What joy!" taught President Spencer W. Kimball. "Those laden with transgressions and sorrows and sin may be forgiven and cleansed and purified if they will return to their Lord, learn of him, and keep his commandments. And all of us needing to repent of day-to-day follies and weaknesses can likewise share in this miracle."[2]

In an article entitled "Roadblocks to Progress," Elder Marvin J. Ashton writes: "Mistakes can be forgiven. Habits can be changed. One more roadblock to progress can be removed. In contrast to this process, how discouraging it is to witness someone who lives with damaging habits and who resists taking personal steps toward better self-management . . . The truly repentant will put their mistakes behind, learn from them, and turn their attention from them to actions that bring progress and growth. How comforting it is to know that God will take us by the hand and lift us to new levels of attitude and achievement if we will but let Him. What a sweet, personal victory it is to recognize misdirection in one's own life and to pay the price that then lets us walk in His paths."[3]

In the words of the Lord himself: "My grace is sufficient for all men that humble themselves before me; for if they humble themselves before me, and have faith in me, then will I make weak things become strong unto them" (Ether 12:27).

"What a promise from the Lord! The very source of our troubles can be changed, molded and formed into a strength and source of power."[4]

Do you believe that the Savior has both the power and the desire to turn your weaknesses into strengths?

<hr />

2. Spencer W. Kimball, *The Miracle of Forgiveness* (Salt Lake City: Bookcraft, 1969), 367-68.
3. Marvin J. Ashton, "Roadblocks to Progress," *Ensign,* May 1979, 67.
4. Ezra Taft Benson, "A Mighty Change of Heart," *Ensign,* Oct. 1989, 2.

Free from the Burden of Sin

> ## Dares to Improve Your Life
>
> - I dare you to use the steps of repentance to rid yourself of burdens you are carrying.
>
> - Beginning today, I dare you to pray each morning and evening that Heavenly Father will help you see the areas of your life that need improving, and to ask for help in doing so.
>
> - For a week, I dare you to study daily about repentance and the Atonement: search the scriptures, read General Conference talks, or a book such as The Miracle of Forgiveness or Believing Christ.
>
> - I dare you to gain a testimony of the power of the Atonement to transform your life, and share it with another person.

A less active man confessed to his bishop that the greatest obstacle to his returning to activity was that he felt too ashamed of the things he had done and didn't see any way that God could ever forgive him.

The spiritually sensitive bishop opened a discussion with the man about the gravity of his sins and whether they required confession to a bishop. Then he opened his scriptures and read from the prophet Isaiah: "Come now, and let us reason together, saith the Lord: though your sins be as scarlet, they shall be as white as snow; though they be red like crimson, they shall be as wool." Then he explained, "The Lord is saying, it doesn't matter what you've done, I can erase it and make you clean again."

The power of the Atonement to restore and change lives is illustrated in the life of Alma the Younger. Before his rebirth, he was described as "a very wicked and an idolatrous man" (Mosiah 27:8). Mormon wrote he was "the vilest of sinners" (Mosiah 28:4). Yet the infinite and eternal Atonement of Jesus Christ applied to him as it applies to each of us.

Alma testified, "As I was thus racked with torment, while I was harrowed up by the memory of my many sins, behold, I remembered also to have heard my father prophesy unto the people concerning the coming of one Jesus Christ, a Son of God, to atone for the sins of the world. Now, as my mind caught hold upon this thought, I cried within my heart: O Jesus, thou Son of God, have mercy on me, who am in the gall of bitterness, and am encircled about by the everlasting chains of death. And now, behold when I thought this, I could remember my pains no more; yea, I was harrowed up by the memory of my sins no more. And oh, what joy, and what marvelous light I did behold; yea, my soul was filled with joy as exceeding as was my pain!" (Alma 36:17-20).

Too many become discouraged because they cannot make their mortal selves behave perfectly. They have forgotten or do not understand that we are on a journey toward perfection and that mistakes will be made. By turning to the Savior, we can be cleansed, consoled, and given strength to keep moving forward. "This is what the gospel is all about," wrote President Gordon B. Hinckley, "to make bad men good and good men better."[1]

President Ezra Taft Benson counseled, "We must take our sins to the Lord in humble and sorrowful repentance. We must plead with Him for power to overcome them. The promises are sure. He will come to our aid. We will find the power to change our lives . . . as we seek to become more and more godlike, [we must be careful] that we do not become discouraged and lose hope. Becoming Christlike is a lifetime pursuit and very often involves growth and change that is slow, almost imperceptible."[2]

"No one has been sent to earth to fail," stated President Howard W. Hunter. "No one has come into this second estate who does not have the capacity to return to God honorably and, with him, enjoy peace and glory everlasting."[3]

Do you believe Jesus Christ has the power to cleanse your sins?

---

1. Gordon B. Hinckley, *Be Thou an Example* (Salt Lake City: Deseret Book Co., 1981), 68.
2. Ezra Taft Benson, "A Mighty Change of Heart," *Ensign*, October 1989, 2.
3. Howard W. Hunter, *That We Might Have Joy,* (Salt Lake City: Deseret Book Co., 1994), 20.

Index